Keto Diet Book for Beginners UK 2021

The Ultimate Keto Diet Cookbook Guide to Boost Your Immune System with Quick, Easy and Delicious Ketogenic Recipes. Keto Recipe Book with 21 Day Action Plan and Success Journal.

Author: Sarah Thomas

TABLE OF CONTENTS

Hey there!

I would like to thank you for your trust and I really hope you'll enjoy the book.

A lot of thought and effort went into creating the book. I am not a part of a big publishing company and I take care of the whole publishing process myself in an effort to make sure your cooking journey is as smooth as possible.

If for any reason you did not like the book you can write on my email at deliciousrecipes.publishing@gmail.com. I always make sure to get back to everybody and if you're not happy with the book I can share another cookbook or two with you for free.

I'm trying really hard to create the best cookbooks I can and I'm always open to constructive criticism.

Enjoy!

Fundamentals of the Keto Diet

The Ketogenic or Keto Diet is a high fat and low carb subset of the overall arch of low carb diets. It is said that a keto diet is great for weight loss as it can transform your body into a lean, mean, fat-burning machine. It does this by directing the body to a state of ketosis, during which the body is forced to utilize fats for energy instead of carbs. In order to force the body to utilize fats, a person on a ketogenic diet must consume lower amounts of carbohydrates, with a high amount of fat and sufficient amounts of proteins. By eating this way, we allow our bodies to fall into a state known as ketosis, stimulating the liver's breakdown of fat cells into ketones and fatty acids which in turn results in weight loss.

How Does the Ketogenic Diet Work?
The ketogenic diet, unlike most popular fad diets, does not rely solely on calorie reduction or starving to death. Instead, it focuses greatly on reallocating calories from one food group to another, primarily from carbs to healthy fats, which, in turn, leads to more energy being burnt than that which is consumed. This results in losing weight and maintaining a lower weight long term.

You may be wondering why the keto diet focuses on reducing complex carbs versus lowering the number of calories taken in like other diets. The reason is that the diet focuses on a healthy sustainable lifestyle instead of cutting calories and starving yourself to death which is not sustainable and makes the whole process a lot less enjoyable. The idea is that if you can train your body to have proper hunger control, it would be far more effective than starving yourself. If you dislike counting calories for every meal the ketogenic diet is a great option.

Everything we eat is categorized into a variety of smaller groups known as macronutrients, or macros for short. The three main macros are fats, carbohydrates, and proteins. If you want to reach Ketosis, then you really need to pay close attention to your macros. Too many carbs and you'll blow your chances, too many proteins and you can really slow the process or stop it all together. We'll discuss macros later on in the book.

How Keto Diet Can Help You?

As mentioned before, what makes the keto diet stand out is the fact that it doesn't focus so much on calorie restriction as with other mainstream diets. Getting your body to a state of ketosis is the main premise of the diet, as this is what aids in you shedding the stubborn fat we often struggle with. While in ketosis, our bodies produce ketones from burning fat which is used for energy. These ketones are formed in the liver from burning the fatty acids found in the food we eat and our existing body fat. The ketones are then used for energy while we shed those unwanted pounds.

Additionally, because the diet is very filling it makes it easier to stick to the diet and not be hungry all the time. This doesn't just help in the beginning when we are very motivated but helps us to maintain the diet once the initial bouts of motivation are gone.

What is Ketosis and How Does it Help You Be Less Hungry?

As stated previously, ketosis is a metabolic state in which the body is forced to utilize fats or ketones for energy instead of the usual carbs. One of the main benefits from being in a state of ketosis is that the macros you are consuming not only kick start your metabolism, prompting weight loss but also energize your organs leaving your stomach feeling full. This mirage of satisfaction leaves you fuller for longer hence requires you to eat less often. Bear in mind that this feeling is based solely on the premise that you utilize the trackers and meet your recommended macro percentages on a daily basis.

Is Remaining in Ketosis safe for the long term?

Yes, it is, however if you are pregnant or have been diagnosed with a chronic illness, it is recommended that you consult a physician to see if the diet is right for you before beginning your keto journey. In the long run, a ketogenic diet can be a safe lifestyle to follow. Although there are many benefits associated with the ketogenic diet, as with all things, it has its drawbacks too. A major disadvantage is that it tends to lead to a fiber deficiency, as carbohydrates are a major source of fiber. This can cause problems, such as constipation, since fiber is important in digestion and excretion. Adding small amounts of wheat bran to your diet can provide you with an extra source of fiber that is low in carbohydrates. Apart from constipation, there can be some minor effects, such as odor from body, breath or sweat.

12 Science-Based Ways to Reduce Hunger and Appetite

Weight loss generally requires you to reduce the number of calories that you consume on a daily basis. The sad part of dieting for weight loss is that restricting calories often leaves us severely hungry with an increased appetite. This can make the whole process severely counterproductive as you end up eating more often causing a larger struggle to lose weight or maintain a healthier weight.

Luckily, there are ways in which we can aid in reducing hunger and appetite that are both based in science and healthy. Twelve such ways are:

1. Ensure you eat a sufficient amount of protein:
Consuming adequate levels of protein will give you a feeling of fullness for longer periods of time. You want the body to utilize your fats for energy which therefore leaves the role of protein to solely help build your muscle mass and help you feel satiated. However, make sure you are not consuming too much protein. Consuming more protein than your body needs can result in your body converting it to glucose which can lead to a high blood sugar levels in your body put you towards an opposite direction of ketosis.

2. Limiting your alcohol intake:
You should already be avoiding alcoholic beverages if you are on any sort of diet since drinking empty calories will make your feel hungry and will not help your weight loss goals.
Another problem with alcohol is our lack of self-discipline that accompanies our drinking behavior. We had a few a few drinks, we're feeling a bit tipsy, we forget about our long term goals, our perception of what's important changes and voila, we're back to eating our favourite junk foods.

3. Filling up on water/carbonated water
Filling up on water might be a good idea, not just as a lifestyle practice, but because it will keep your stomach fuller for longer periods of time. Because the diet plan generally has a diuretic effect, (which releases extra fluid, adding to a person's weight) it is important to become a huge fan of water.

Keep bottles of water around you to remind you to drink up. Also, it is advised that you drink a glass before it's time to eat, which, further (outside of the diet) helps with portion control.

Carbon water has also been proven to help with satiety and feeling of fullness. Drinking carbon water also helps with constipation and digestion which will help with your health and weight loss goals.

4. Use Fenugreek

Fenugreek is a spice that is often used in Indian cooking and some studies have shown that the herb helps with delayed stomach emptying which in turn helps you feel full for longer.

5. Munch on healthy snacks (when needed):

Studies have shown that 'healthy snackers' have less issues with losing weight and feel better about diets.

I get it, I've been there as well, you're watching a movie and having a great time and it would feel even better to get some of your favourite snacks to add to the enjoyment. I've been there plenty of times. Too often I found myself reaching for a candy bar, a couple of cookies, a bag of chips or other forbidden items that are not on the approved Keto list.

Eating keto approved meals will help reduce the occurrence of snack attacks but won't totally eliminate them in the early leg of your journey. So being prepared will help you deal with the temptations to munch and graze when they arise.

Create emergency packs filled with healthy, tasty nuts, meat jerkies, an avocado or other tasty keto snack to tackle the cravings head on when they arise. Doing so will not only aid in you losing pounds, but hep you push a bit longer between your next meals.

6. Adding Red Pepper flakes to your breakfast:

One overlooked ingredient that secretly helps to keep you fuller for longer is red pepper flakes. Eating them early in the day as part of your breakfast or with a midmorning snack has the amazing effect of reducing the amount of food you'll eat later on.They help reduce your appetite and dramatically weaken the otherwise powerful afternoon cravings we're all tempted by.

7. Spray on your dressings or oils instead of pouring:

Investing in a couple of spray bottles could yield as big or even better returns for weight loss than investing in a pricey rowing machine. But like the rowing machine the spray bottles are not going to work if you don't use them.

Decant your dressings and oils into the spray bottle and use them when you are cooking and eating instead of pouring out the oil or dressing from the container. You'll be amazed at how much further they go, how much longer they last, and how much money you'll save.

But most importantly you'll be thrilled at how much weight you are losing. A spray or two of oil is more than enough to cover a pan, and a couple of blasts over a salad will spread the taste far further and use much less dressing than pouring or drizzling will. You'll not notice any difference to your meal - if anything, using less oil will probably make the ingredients taste much better.

You will soon notice the difference the big reduction in the calorie count is making on you!

8. Use Edamame Beans for Munchies:

Edamame is a key ingredient and popular starter in many oriental restaurants, and it should consider adopting it into your diet if you're serious about losing weight.

It's a fancy name for boiled green soybeans still in their pods. They're packed with fiber, protein, vitamins and essential minerals and are great for making you feel full and satiated.

Just half-a-cup-a-day provides the same fiber as four slices of whole-wheat bread and the same amount of iron as a four-ounce chicken breast. They're normally available on the frozen foods section and are a great, low-cost and rather trendy way to snack.

9. Avoid using too much salt:

Salt is a massive contributor to piling on the pounds and for some people it can be one of the bigger reasons why they are finding it so hard to slim down and shed the weight they want to.Because salt makes food so tasty it's almost everywhere and many in the West eat twice the recommended amount daily.

It doesn't cause weight gain; it adds to bloating, hunger and thirst and can really hinder your efforts to lose weight.

Get in a habit of checking for sodium content on food labels and choose fresh foods over packaged foods.
This doesn't mean having to endure mouthfuls of season-less, tasteless food. There are plenty of other alternatives to try that will keep your taste buds buzzing and your meals appetizing.

10.   Start your day off with eggs:
Studies have shown that people who begin their days by having eggs for breakfast feel less hungry in the afternoon than those who ate a carb-heavy morning meal. Eggs are very versatile so pretty much every breakfast can include eggs and still look very different.

11. Aim to get a good night's sleep:
Researchers at Colombia University have found that better sleep leads to better weight loss. Their study compared women who on average only get five hours of sleep a night with women who manage to get seven hours of sleep.
 The results are startling - those who slept only five hours a night are more than twice as likely to be obese as compared to the women who get seven hours of sleep. Sleep deprivation is a cause of stress and stress triggers the release of the fat storage hormone cortisol. Levels of hormones associated with controlling hunger, leptin and ghrelin, are also believed to be affected by sleep deprivation. Insufficient sleep will leave you feeling hungry, less satiated and with a stronger appetite. Combine that with being tired and less alert with a weakened mind and that's a perfect recipe to fall into temptation and start eating unhealthy foods. Aim to get a minimum seven hours sleep and you'll not only feel a whole lot better, but you will also release less cortisol and diminish your hunger.

12. Supplement with L-glutamine
A lot of studies support the fact that glutamine in some cases can quite drastically help with suppressing appetite. L-Glutamine is an amino acid that can be found in foods such as chicken, fish, cabbage, spinach, beans, lentils. You can also supplement with glutamine in order to make sure you get enough of it and reap the benefits.

Is Keto Diet a Heart-Healthy Diet?

The main idea behind the Keto diet is that the distribution of macros leads the body into the metabolic state of ketosis. This in turn pushes the body into a fat burning frenzy combatting obesity and other chronic illnesses on its path to weight loss.

As such, any amount weight you lose on the keto diet can aid in lessening the risk factor of cardiovascular rated illnesses such as hypertension, diabetes, obesity, and regulating cholesterol levels. All of which aids in preventing heart disease.

By reducing inflammation and oxidative stress a ketogenic diet can definitely be considered a heart-healthy diet.

Benefits of Keto Diet

The Ketogenic diet has been responsible for improving millions of lives across the globe. These benefits include, but are not limited to:

- **Clearer Thinking**

The mental cloud that accompanies a high carbohydrate diet disappears. When the body enters ketosis, a steady flow of ketones travels to the brain. This is due to the fact that the keto diet removes the onset of intense sugar cravings. The additional energy reserved from the removed craving and functions of the brain and organs results in increased levels of concentration as well as improved focus.

While this is an amazing benefit, it is only right to note that there have also been a few people who have been fully cured from apnea after transitioning to the keto diet and reducing complex carbs from their diet.

- ### Losing Weight / Maintaining a Healthy Weight

Most of the people are suffering from the problem of extra weight and many of them are scared of obesity that is why experts have been constantly looking for a solution that can help people lose weight in healthy way. And the Ketogenic diet proved to be one of the best ways to stay fit and have a great shape. And because the Ketogenic diet is sugar-free, high in fats and low in carbohydrates, the body will start using it as its primary source of energy. Hence, if you want a diet that can help you lose weight in a short time; the Ketogenic diet will be the best choice you can opt for and you will be surprised by the amount of fat you will start to lose.

- ### Boosting Energy & Your Ability to Focus

The Ketogenic diet can help provide you with more energy by boosting the level of fats in your blood. Your system will be able to break the fats it receives from proteins. Adopting a ketogenic diet also helps your mind focus better and it has been proven that keto diet helps treating drug-resistant epilepsy in children, helps with Alzheimer's disease and improves concentration.

- ### Appetite Control

When you adopt a diet that is high in carbohydrates, you will feel hungry very soon after each meal.
On the contrary, when you start eating more protein and fats your body will naturally start feeling less hungry and it will be a lot easier for you to control your appetite.

- ### Improving HDL Cholesterol & Blood Pressure Levels

The Ketogenic diet has proven its ability to improve the level of triglyceride in your blood and helps controls the cholesterol levels. Following a Ketogenic lifestyle allows the blood to flow better through your body. It allows an important increase in good cholesterol and helps lower the level of bad cholesterol LDL.

- **Preventing / Relieving Epilepsy**

The Keto diet has always been used as a control mechanism for epilepsy since the 1900s. And until today, the Ketogenic diet is widely used to help control the epileptic condition of children. And following a Ketogenic diet will help epileptic people reduce the use of their medications.

What are Macros and How to Count them?

Macro is short for macronutrient and there's three categories: Carbohydrates, Proteins and Fats.

You can count the macros on your own but it's very easy to not do things correctly especially if this is the first time you are doing it. That's why I feel that the simplest, quickest and the most accurate way is to download a macro tracking app.
When you just start out on a Keto diet, one of the first things you should do is search around for a reputable Keto calculator app to help you get to and remain in ketosis. One such app that prevailed in the top lists of 2020 and early 2021 is Carb Manager.

Once downloaded, the app will ask you to enter general information used for weight management, similar to what is done in the 21 Day Success Journal featured below, such as your age, gender, weight, height, activity level, body fat percentage. This helps them to determine if your goal should be weight loss or to simply maintenance. Following which it gives you a safe space to track useful Keto metrics such as blood sugar levels, ketones, macronutrients and so much more.

The calculator will also provide you will the exact number of fats, carbs, and proteins you should be eating a day based on the information you provided. Once you have calculated your particular needs, you will have a clear idea of how to plan your meals going forward.

Carb Manager also acts as a great food journaling app as it allows you to scan, enter or create all the foods, drink, or vitamins you've consumed throughout the day. This log helps you to see where you are in turns of your daily macros.

Speaking of which, let's take a few minutes to discuss macronutrients which will be vital for you to watch allow your road to ketosis and ongoing weight loss journey.

Important Macros on The Keto Diet

Carbs	Recommended percentage of carbs on a Keto diet: 5% - 10%.
	Carbohydrates are the most recognized as "starchy" foods such as bread, pasta, potatoes, and rice. Carbohydrates also include sugars and sugar-containing foods such as fruit, candy, cakes, alcohol etc. As soon as the amount of sugar in the blood is raised, your pancreas gets the message to pump out more insulin, so the blood sugar can be processed and moved around the body as energy.
Fats	Recommended percentage of **healthy** fats on a Keto diet: 55% - 60%.
	Fat is the teacher's pet of the Ketogenic diet. Most of your daily meals will be made up of fats. This can sometimes be a hard thing to get your head around, because "fat" can often be ruled out as "bad" and something to be avoided but that is not true. There are 3 main types of fat: saturated, monounsaturated, and polyunsaturated. Instead of confusing you with a rundown of these 3 fats, I will provide you with this tip instead: Fats which are "whole" or "from the source" such as eggs, grass-fed meats, heavy cream, butter, fresh fatty fish such as salmon are all healthy sources of fat.
	Products which have been processed and refined down to a "different" form than how they started are "bad" fats, such as margarine and vegetable oils, apart from olive oil. If you are unsure if a fatty food is okay or not, just think: is this in a package with lots of ingredients and scientific words? Has it been processed to the extent where it comes in a different form from where it

	started? If so, then avoid it. If you can say, "this food hasn't been processed, it is reasonably close to its original form, and the ingredients list is very short," then go ahead and add it to your list.
Protein	Recommended percentage of protein on a Keto diet: 30% - 35%.

Handling protein amounts on the keto diet can be tricky as it has the potential of converting to glucose if too much of it is consumed. That's why it is of extreme importance that you adhere to the recommended percentages.

Going over the percentages on a regular basis can cause your body start burning glucose for energy, instead of fat, essentially ruining ketosis. On the other hand, if you adhere to above percentages your muscles and tissues will use the protein accumulated from maintenance and growth instead of burning it for energy and storing unwanted fat. |

How to Prepare Delicious Recipes to Keep "Cheating"?

Many dieters believe that snacking or indulging on delicious foods is somehow considered cheating. They are forgetting that key ingredient to a successful diet is 'consistency'. We need to make sure we are consistent in our efforts and make sure our diet is sustainable. One of the great things about the keto diet is that there are ways to create delicious recipes to make the feeling of cheating okay, when you experience the munchies. Outside of using up all the herbs and spices available to you to make your meals even more delicious, you can also allow yourself the leverage to indulge in keto approved snacks.

I know, it may seem difficult to think that snacking is possible on a keto diet, but there are actually tons of options when it comes to low-carb snacks. Maybe you want snack ideas for your busy days, or perhaps, you would like a homemade Sunday snack after dinner. Either way, we've got fresh and creative recipes below that are sure to meet your cravings.

- **Quest Bars:**

If you were looking for the ultimate go-to ketogenic snack, you've found it in these small, delicious Quest Bar snacks. With no added sugars and a net carb value of only 3-4 grams makes it a perfect keto snack. Apart from the fact that they they're definitely low in carbs, they come in several different flavors, such as my favorites, the Chocolate Chip Cookie Dough, and the Peanut Butter Supreme.

- **Beef Jerky:**

Beef Jerky is tasty, low in carbs, and is conveniently packaged for on the go. However, the ones found "off the shelf" tend to be higher in carbohydrates. A compromise would be the Old Wisconsin Snack Sticks, which are both flavorful and impressively low in carbs. The great news is that you can get the sticks in the UK as well, I usually just order them from Amazon.

- **Pepperoni Slices:**

They're good all by themselves, but with added cheese, they're irresistible. Remember to watch out for calorie limits, because these snacks can definitely rack up calories.

- **Cold Cuts and Cheese Roll-Ups:**

All you need is a slice of cheese and your favourite meat and you got yourself another delicious low-carb snack. Whether it be turkey, roast beef or ham, you're sure to enjoy it to the last bite!

- **Hard Boiled Eggs:**

Some people might not consider this a low carb snack, but I do. I love some hard-boiled eggs from time to time that keep me full because they contain a lot of the essential amino acid called L-glutamine that was mentioned before. Hard-boiled eggs are healthy, quick, simple and convenient snacks.

- **Low Carb Bars:**

With improved taste that brings a natural, flavorful appeal, low carb bars have become another great option. No longer do they have such a strong, undesirable "artificial sugar" taste, but they have a much better taste with different added flavors. My favourites are Chocolate Hazelnut, Peanut Butter Fudge Crisp, Caramel Nut Chew and Cookies N' Crem.

- **Small Salad:**

Salads are a great choice, no matter how you toss them together-whether you simply like your mixed greens with olive oil, or you prefer more variety, such as meat, cheese and hard-boiled eggs, more filling.

- **Peanuts:**

While peanuts are a bit tricky, since they can cause trouble if you overindulge, when eaten in smaller portions, they prove to be a great snack. Having a net carb value of 3g per quarter cup, it's not bad once you monitor your ketogenic limits.

- **Almonds:**

With less than 2.5g of net carbs per quarter cup, almonds make an excellent snack option.

Top 5 Tips to Control Cholesterol and Lose Weight

1. Watch your Sodium Intake:

Consuming a high amount of sodium can increase your blood pressure and cholesterol. So, try to regulate your intake of sodium and focus on a regular intake of nutrients such as magnesium, calcium and potassium which offer an array of benefits.

2. Add Regular Exercise to your Routine:

The keto diet should be combined with physical activities that will assist in lowering your cholesterol, increasing metabolism and boosting immunity. Prepare a routine and include physical exercises that will keep you in good shape and burn unwanted calories.

3. Track your Goals & Reward your Successes:

What gets tracked, gets analyzed and what gets analyzed can be improved and optimized. It all starts with tracking. Sometimes we're not in touch with objective reality of the situation and think we're eating better than we really are so it's important to track your food intake.

You have a long journey ahead so do make sure you reward yourself for the milestones you reach with non-food treats. The milestones do not have to be big, set up small milestones for which you can reward yourself and that will keep you motivated.

4. Consider Keeping a Macro Journal:

Practice the habit of going through nutrition labels so you are aware of what you are eating and jot down your daily macros. This will not only aid in you getting to or maintaining a state of ketosis, but also avoid foods that will increase your cholesterol.

5. Seek Support:

Seek assistance from doctors, friends, or physicians if you are having a hard time sticking to the diet plan. Counseling and support sessions will boost your morale and confidence and will provide room for further improvement.

Approved Food List

There are a large variety of foods you can enjoy on the keto diet. Let's dive into to some examples of foods you can enjoy on the keto diet and also talk about the foods you should avoid

What foods can you eat on Keto Diet?
When it comes to listing what's allowed, I like to break things down into two categories:
- Foods you can enjoy on a daily basis
- Food you can enjoy occasionally, 1 – 3 servings a week for most of them.

Foods You Can Enjoy Often
1. Healthy Fats

These are fats that can be used for cooking. Such as:

- Lard
- Goose fat
- Macadamia oil
- Butter
- Coconut oil
- Duck fat
- Olive oil
- Tallow
- Avocado oil
- Chicken fat
- Clarified butter or ghee

2. Animal Based Proteins

Of course, the vegetarian and vegan diet does not include meat, poultry or fish. Therefore, you will get your protein through other foods and supplements:

- Seitan
- Non-Dairy Butter
- Tofu
- Lentils
- Chickpeas
- Vegan Protein Powder

3. Fruits

Unfortunately, most fruits are excluded from this list because of their high sugar content. However, you can still often enjoy:

- Avocado (often thought of as vegetable but biologically it is considered a fruit)
- Raspberries
- Strawberries
- Lemons

There's a few other fruits that are considered low carb but it's better to keep the list short and rather be safe than sorry.

4. Beverages and Condiments

Regarding beverages, try to avoid those with artificial sweeteners, additives, soy lecithin and hormones. Instead, drink/eat:

- Water
- Pesto
- Pickles
- Kimchi
- Whey protein
- Coffee, sweetened with natural milk or black
- Bone broth
- Mustard
- Tea, herbal or black
- Kombucha
- Sauerkraut
- Lime juice and zest

5. Non-Starchy Vegetables

Contrary to common belief, all veggies are not equal. There are some that are remarkably high in carbohydrates. However, below is a list of those that are lower in carbohydrates, which you can consume as often as you like.

- Chard
- Bamboo shoots
- Radishes
- Bok choy
- Chives
- Endive
- Spaghetti squash
- Dark leaf kale
- Cucumber
- Kohlrabi
- Celery stalk
- Asparagus
- Zucchini
- Swiss chard
- Spinach
- Radicchio
- Lettuce

Foods You Can Eat Occasionally:

1. Fruits

As previously mentioned, most fruits are too high in sugar content to be regularly enjoyed, but occasionally, you can enjoy:

- Blackberries
- Olives
- Blueberries
- Mulberries
- Cranberries
- Coconut

2. Vegetables, Fruits, and Mushrooms

Every now and again, you can indulge in the following:

- Turnips
- Rutabaga
- Eggplant
- Tomatoes
- Peppers
- Parsley root
- Spring onion
- Leek
- Bean sprouts
- Sugar snap peas
- Wax beans
- Artichokes
- Water chestnuts
- Rhubarb
- White and green cabbage
- Red cabbage
- Cauliflower
- Broccoli
- Brussels sprouts
- Fennel
- Onion
- Garlic
- Mushrooms
- Pumpkin
- Nori
- Kombu
- Okra

3. Full Fat Dairy:

Although dairy is known to be a danger zone for most diets, in the ketogenic diet, full-fat dairy is permitted. This would mean, though, that you need to ensure that the product is really full-fat, or high-fat, rather than being labelled "low – fat". Products with this label tend to be filled with sugars, starch, and artificial additives. The full fat dairy products to consume:

- Heavy cream
- Sour cream
- Cheese
- Plain yogurt
- Cottage cheese

4. Condiments:

These condiments can be enjoyed occasionally if they are sugar-free:

- Tomato puree
- Passata

5. Seeds and Nuts:

Seeds and nuts are a great if you are on a ketogenic diet and they can actually be eaten more than 1 – 3 times a week.

- Almonds
- Walnuts
- Pumpkin seeds
- Hazelnuts
- Flaxseed
- Hemp seeds
- Macadamia nuts
- Pecans
- Pine nuts
- Sesame seeds
- Sunflower seeds
- Brazil nuts

6. Fermented Soy Products

If not genetically modified or processed, fermented soy products are permitted occasionally. Including:

- Tamari
- Coconut aminos
- Edamame
- Natto
- Tempeh
- Black soybean

7. Chocolate and Desserts:

Sugar-free desserts that do not have a large amount of carbs can be enjoyed every now and then. However, you should avoid soy lecithin when checking the ingredient list. For chocolate, the darker it is, the more natural it is, so, use this rule of thumb in addition to checking ingredient lists.

- Chocolate, extra dark
- Cocoa powder
- Cocoa
- Carob powder

8. Healthy sweeteners:

Once in a while, refined sugars can be replaced with healthy sweeteners. However, these products must be all-natural:

- Swerve
- Erythritol
- Stevia

9. Thickeners:

The following can be used from time to time to thicken soups and sauces:

- Xanthan gum
- Arrowroot powder

What food can't you eat on Keto Diet?

The foods mentioned below should ideally not be eaten. If you do decide to indulge from time to time, make sure you do it very sparingly.

- Sweetened juices
- Grains
- Honey, syrup or sugar in any form
- Starchy vegetables
- Most store-bought baked goods
- Sweetened yogurt
- High-sugar fruits
- Chips and crackers

It is vital that you keep in mind that these foods should be avoided and that you should be more creative with your 'cheat' meals. Try to make your favourite recipes with keto ingredients.

The Ultimate Keto Shopping List

Protein

- Cod
- Bacon
- Shellfish
- Lobster
- Shrimp
- Beef
- Low Carb Burgers
- Swordfish
- Sea Bass
- Chicken
- Oysters
- Tofu
- Eggs
- Tuna
- Pork
- Red Snapper
- Elk
- Turkey
- Flounder
- Sardine
- Salmon
- Grouper
- Herring
- Turkey Bacon
- Sausage
- Lamb
- Turkey Sausage
- Scallops
- Sea Bass
- Liver

Healthy Fats

- Sunflower Oil
- Avocado
- Coconut Oil
- MCT Oil
- Avocado Oil
- Ghee
- Unsalted Butter
- Olive Oil

Nuts

- High-Fat Snacks Almonds,
- Natural Almond Walnuts
- Sesame Seeds
- Pumpkin Seeds, unsalted
- Macadamia Nuts

Diary

- Cheese, all types, full fat
- Whole Milk
- Greek Yogurt, unsweetened
- Unsweetened Coconut Milk
- Unsweetened Almond Milk
- Unsweetened Cashew Milk

Other/Condiments

- Lemon Juice
- Lime Juice
- Soy Sauce
- Apple Cider
- Low Sodium Soy Sauce
- White Wine Vinegar
- Balsamic Vinegar
- Red Wine Vinegar
- Red Pepper Flakes

Vegetables

- Onions
- Chives
- Radishes
- Artichokes
- Parsnips
- Arugula
- Cilantro
- Cucumbers
- Snow Peas
- Collard Greens
- Broccoli
- Asparagus
- Bell Peppers
- Eggplant
- Scallion
- Bok Choy
- Spinach
- Celeriac
- Leeks
- Watercress
- Romaine Lettuce
- Acorn Squash
- Brussels Sprouts
- Endive
- Fennel
- Butternut Squash
- Tomatoes
- Ginger
- Carrots
- Cabbage
- Turmeric
- Mushrooms
- Green Beans
- Kale
- Okra
- Turnips
- Cauliflower
- Zucchini
- Celery
- Chicory
- Chili Peppers
- Mustard Green

Top 5 Keto Diet Mistakes You Must Avoid

1. Drinking Alcohol on A Regular Basis

Alcohol causes changes in the way your body stores energy from food which in turn makes it very hard to lose weight. Therefore, if you're on a ketogenic diet, alcohol should be avoided as much as possible. Additionally, drinking empty calories will leave you feeling hungry and the lack of self-discipline while intoxicated will make it easier for you to eat the food you shouldn't. Now and then, you can indulge in a little bit of clear spirits with carb free diet mixers, but within the first two weeks of your diet, don't consume alcohol at all.

2. Not Drinking Enough Water

Studies have shown that most of the people in the UK are dehydrated. Drinking enough water will not only help with weight loss but also provides a whole lot of other health benefits and increased energy throughout the day.

3. Eating Too Much Protein

While on a Keto diet it is vital that you moderate the amount of protein that you consume. You want the body to utilize your fats for energy which therefore leaves the role of protein to solely help build your muscle mass. Consuming more protein than your body needs can result in your body converting it to glucose which can lead to a high blood sugar content in your body and in the opposite direction of ketosis.

4. Going to a Grocery Store Unprepared

If you go to a grocery store without a plan and a mental heads up that you will only buy the food you are supposed it will be very easy for you to rationalize the purchases of bad foods. First, it will start with an occasional purchase and before you know it you will be back to your bad habits. Always a shopping list ready and try to be in and out of store as soon as possible if you are struggling with this particular aspect of the keto lifestyle.

5. <u>Not Eating Enough Fats or Eating 'Unhealthy' Fats</u>

You are allowed to eat a good portion of fats on the keto diet, but that doesn't mean you can eat any fats you want. It is important for you to consume mostly healthy fats if you intend on losing those unwanted pounds.

The keto diet is meant to be high fat as this is what your body will be converting into energy hence it is vital that you hit your daily fat macros in order to potentially lose fat.

How Keto Diet Helps to Boost Your Immune System

Over the past few years more and more data has come out that shows that keto diet significantly improves the immune system, hence helping combat common illnesses.

One example is a recent study where the scientists placed a set of mice on the keto diet and compared them to a second set who ate a regular diet to see how the diet affected their immune system and their body's reaction to common viruses. The results showed that the mice on the keto diet were less likely to contract the common virus like influenza.

Upon further investigation it was determined that this was due to the protective effect of the body being in ketosis on the keto diet. While in this state the body was able to produce more gamma-delta T cells inside the lungs of the mice eating the keto diet. The additional T cells encouraged the production of more mucus in the epithelial cells that, in turn, aided in containing the virus.

Keto Diet and Diabetes

One major issue affecting people that are currently overweight, struggling with PCOS or who simply don't eat well is the onset of diabetes. Diabetes is essentially caused by the bodies inability to handle, properly produce and regulate insulin. The degree of insulin resistance determines whether you would be classified as prediabetic, suffering from type I diabetes or a type II diabetes patient.

A ketogenic diet can aid in lowering your blood sugar levels and maintaining a more consistent blood glucose level. This will in turn aid in regulating the level of insulin produced and stored in the body. Hereby assisting in the prevention or regulation of diabetes.

Keto Diet for Seniors

As we age, our bodies and its nutritional needs change. A senior transitioning to keto diet would therefore benefit from a variety of perks associated with the keto diet.

Before we dive into what some of these benefits are, it is important to note that you should consider consulting a medical professional who is knowledgeable about your current medical conditions and can determine if the keto diet would be best for you before taking the plunge into the lifestyle.

Okay, now that you have received the green light from your doctor. Here are a few things you may benefit from when transitioning to a keto diet as a senior:

- Easier Weight Loss

The more we age, the harder it becomes to lose weight. This can be due to higher stress levels, slower metabolism rate and rapid loss of muscle. The keto diet offers the perfect solution by burning fat at a higher rate.

- Deeper & Longer Sleep

Many seniors suffer from a variety of sleep disorders including, but not limited to, sleep apnea, insomnia, sleepwalking, and restless leg syndrome. Eating the macros allotted on the keto diet will encourage the body to indulge in adenosine activity leaving the body more relaxed and creating favorable conditions for deeper and longer sleep, with less disturbances.

- Avoiding the Onset of Chronic Diseases

The Keto diet has been said to help reduce the risks for a variety of chronic diseases, including but not limited to, diabetes, Parkinson's Disease, cancer, cardiovascular diseases, mental disorders, multiple sclerosis and fatty liver disease.

Strategy and Tactics for Keto Success

How to Make a Personalized Plan that Works for You

Achieving the right balance of proteins, carbohydrates, fats and calories can be difficult for a keto or low-carb dieter. To assist you in keeping up with your daily food consumption and meal planning, we have developed a meal planner that is easy to use. With the Ketogenic Diet Planner, you can:

- Monitor macronutrients, such as Proteins, Carbohydrates and Fats in grams, g for each meal or full day.
- Strike the right balance among the previously mentioned macronutrients.

By convention, it is recommended that 60% of caloric intake is from fats, 35% covers protein, and the other 5%, comes from carbohydrates. Not only can you tailor these values, using your diet planner, but you can set a range of values, rather than using a fixed figure. Practicality is important when it comes to proper dieting.

You can follow up on your caloric intake goals, ensuring that you stay within range. Apart from informing you on whether or not you've met your diet goals, your planner will give you a total caloric count and percentage of calories consumed, of daily total amount. This value is found by averaging the highest and lowest target points.

How to Meal Prep Quickly and Efficiently

Many people often confuse the terms "Meal Planning" and "Meal Prep" with some even using them interchangeably. Doing so is a vital error, however, as these terms refer to two completely different concepts.

To Meal Plan, as the name suggests is to plan your meals, nothing more, nothing less. It is basically you sitting down and deciding what meals you will be preparing for a given timeframe (generally a week). It involves no actual prep or additional action.

Meal Prepping, on the other hand, takes the concept and kicks it into action. It involves taking your Meal Plan and actually preparing each meal over the course of a few hours then portioning individual servings into containers to be eaten throughout the week. It is important to note, however, that it is not possible to successfully Meal Prep without first coming up with a successful Meal Plan.

As with all new things, Meal Prep can be daunting when first starting out so, don't feel bad if you need to gauge yourself in the first week. Maybe start with prepping two or three recipes to start then slowly ramp it up as the weeks go on. Your speed of your journey is completely up to you just be sure to keep the following key dos and don'ts in mind as you go forward.

How to Make Keto Diet a Lifestyle

The Keto way of life is more of a lifestyle change than a diet as the adjustments you make while on this diet should stick with you throughout the rest of your life. But how do you make that a reality?
 It's important that you accept this diet as a lifestyle and realize that you will not be on this diet just a few months and that you are interested in a healthy lifestyle for the long term.
Write down your goals on a piece of paper and write down why it is important for you to make the keto diet into a lifestyle so you dig deeper, increase motivation and make a bigger commitment. I would also recommend writing out all the positives that will come from embracing this lifestyle and all the negatives that will happen if you do not follow through. This will make sure you are motivated by both positive and negative

thoughts which is a scientifically proven way of increasing motivation which a lot of performance and motivational coaches teach. If your mindset doesn't change, nothing will.

Below, I have outlined some major health habits that will help your ketogenic diet journey.

A few concepts that will help you:

❖ Hydrating:

Drinking plenty of water will not only help with weight loss but better health and energy as well. Keep bottles of water around you to remind you to drink up or even set up notifications on your find to remind you to drink water until the habit is formed.

❖ Reading Food Labels:

In an effort to monitor carbohydrates as closely as you can, make it a practice to read the labels of the foods that you purchase. The foods allowed on this diet also contain carbs, so be vigilant in your counting to avoid any masked sugars.

❖ Say 'No' to take out:

You may not be the fanciest cook, but enjoying home cooked meals is a major benefit, even for a novice cook. Even if you start by cooking meat and fish, and steaming vegetables, you would be better off with such whole foods than if you had chosen a processed meal which is generally flooded with carbs and other ingredients that do not support your health.

How to Stay Consistent with the Diet

Remaining consistent on the keto diet can be difficult on some days for no other reason than that you are human, and temptations happen. The previously mentioned mental exercise of digging deep into your goals will help you stay disciplined on the days where you want to break your diet.

Here are one of the three most common mistakes that you should avoid if you want to make sure you are consistent with your diet.

1) Not going over your allotted macros

Your macro allotment will be unique to you based on your weight loss goals, current weight, and level of activity. Most keto calculators give you a daily macro target when you start. This number changes as you lose weight to ensure a continuous loss.

2) Setting Drastic or Unrealistic Goals

We all like to believe that we will be the next great miracle of the new the keto diet and lose 100 pounds in our first month. Chances are goals like these will potentially be unattainable and have a negative impact on your weight loss. So, it is better to keep your expectations as realistic as possible. If you want to set up really high goals make sure you give yourself a big enough time frame as well.

The keto diet, if done correctly, has the potential to assist you in your weight loss journey, increase your body's sensitivity to insulin, and regulate the rate in which your body secretes growth hormones, which are all wonderful benefits. However, if you set really high goals, it is important that you also keep in mind that the diet plan is just one aspect of the many things you will need to adjust in your life to achieve success in your body's overall health. You will also need to adjust your overall level of activity, amount of sleep and stress levels for even faster fat loss.

3) Avoid comparing your progress to someone else's journey.

It's important that you understand that everybody is different. Your specific goals may be different from even your spouse, and as such will need to listen to your body and tweak your diet, and activity levels accordingly.

1) Can a vegetarian succeed on a keto diet?

Of course! The keto diet focuses on high fat not animal based protein. If you are a vegetarian simply fill the protein allotment from your macros with keto- friendly plant-based protein sources.

2) What vegetables should I eat?

Vegetables, though safe, should also be weighed and bargained, as you would want to choose veggies of lowest carbs and most nutrition. Of the many that will comprise your carbohydrate quota, the green, leafy veggies are an absolute best.

These include all types of lettuce and cabbage, kale, watercress, spinach, brussel sprouts, radishes, celery, cucumber, bean sprouts, asparagus, cauliflower, and broccoli. However, there are more sugary vegetables, such as onions, tomatoes, peppers and potatoes (or other starchy veggies) that you should ensure that you eat only in minimal amounts.

3) Are there any safety considerations or possible side effects of the keto diet?

Although Keto dieting has been proven to have many health and weight-loss benefits, a sudden or abrupt transition can cause a few mild, short-term effects.

These include:

- **Constipation**

A common mistake that ketogenic dieters make is to forget about fiber when it comes to their daily carb intake. A negative effect of insufficient amounts of fiber is constipation, which can be avoided by eating more green vegetables. In addition to these veggies, it is important to drink lots of water to prevent or help treat constipation. If you still find trouble treating your constipation, you can use a mild over-the-counter laxative to get rid of your problem.

- **Leg Cramps**

It is not unusual to have leg cramps when just starting the keto diet, especially with most instances occurring in the night time. Stemming from a lack of potassium, such cramps can be remedied by taking potassium-containing multivitamins. Whether or not you experience such side effects, the taking of multivitamins is encouraged to prevent deficiencies that may be caused by the diet's restrictions.

- **Bad Breath**

On a keto diet, your body burns fat for energy release, a process we have been referring to as ketosis. As a part of this process, ketones are released in your breath and urine, and acetone, a particular ketone, possesses a specific smell. While the smell of acetone isn't necessarily malodorous (like in the case of bad or smelly breath that is caused by halitosis), you may notice a fruity or sugary smell. If you find it unpleasant, you can just use parsley, fresh mint, breath spray, sugar-free gum, or mouthwash, any of which would do the trick.

4) <u>What is a carbohydrate and how does it affect the diet?</u>

Carbs are made of compounds such as sugars, starches and celluloses. Foods such as bread, rice, potato, pasta and other high carb foods, comprise of starches and other molecules that are more structurally complex. These foods, which are made up of several sugar chains, are acted upon by the enzyme amylase. Amylase in the stomach and saliva break down these carbohydrates into sugars, after which they are digested by the body. Proof of this mechanism would be found in bread, which comprises of starch that is broken down into sugars by salivary amylase. After chewing bread for an extended period of time, you can taste the slight sweetness as evidence of sugars. For you, this would mean greater scrutiny when it comes your carb count, as foods with sugars and starches contain carbohydrates as well. Foods that contain large amounts of sugars and starches should be avoided altogether. Therefore, foods like sweet vegetables (e.g. carrots and peppers), starchy vegetables (e.g., potatoes, swede, yams), starchy foods (e.g. pasta, bread, pastry and rice), and fruit should mostly be excluded from your ketogenic diet.

5) What are Ketostix?

Ketostix are very little strips made of thin cuts of plastic, having a small section designated for reagents. When immersed in urine, or run through a flow of urine, the Ketostix changes color, based on the quantity of ketones present. A positive indication of the presence of ketones confirms ketosis, as well as successful diet results.

6) Do I Have to Buy Ketostix?

This can be answered with both a yes and a no. Its purpose to dieters can be broken down into two major categories:

- **Troubleshooting:**

If you've just started out, you may find your Ketostix incredibly handy, as every minute, you would be anxious to know if you're making good headway. Your Ketostix would let you know if, by your carb cutting, you have achieved ketosis, and are burning fat, as opposed to carbohydrates.
If you are more experienced with the keto diet, you may want to know your limits with carbs before you're no longer in ketosis. Many use the Ketostix for determining this, as well as the ways in which various foods affect ketosis. For instance, there are persons whose bodies can tolerate sugar alcohols in ketosis. Using the Ketostix for this purpose, one can find clarity and diagnosis regarding such tolerance.

- **Psychological Motivation:**

A color change on your Ketostix may not seem like a big deal, but it is definitely true that encouragement sweetens labor. Sometimes, it only takes a little affirmation to keep us going. The ketogenic journey can sometimes be rough, so any sign of making progress is welcomed.

7) Where can I buy Ketostix?

You can find Ketostix Ketone Urinalysis strips in most pharmacies or you can make an online purchase on Amazon, which is my personal preference. Apart from the fact that it is, of course, the more convenient option, I've found that online prices are generally lower.

21 Day Meal Plan

Let's explore a sample 21 Day Meal Plan using the recipes from the book. There are over 100 delicious recipes in the sections that follow so please feel free to mix and match recipes to suit your personal taste and scenarios.

Remember this meal plan is meant to be regarded for informational purposes only. Everybody is different as such their needs and speed of weight loss may differ. So be sure to speak to a medical professional to be sure this meal plan would be best for you.

Day	Breakfast	Lunch	Dinner	Dessert
1	English Scrambled Eggs	Creamy Scallops	Shrimp & Mushrooms	Almond Fat Bombs
2	Parmesan Omelette	Snapper Taco Bowl	Buttery Garlic Turkey	Root Beer Float
3	Egg Filled Avocado	Parmesan Beef Roast	Salmon Boards	Blackberry Shake
4	Almond Pancakes	Turkey Skewers with Peanut Sauce	Steak Bibimbap	Cocoa Fat bomb
5	Strawberries & Cream	Cod Quesadillas	Beef Burger with Sriracha Mayo	Almond Fat Bombs
6	English Scrambled Eggs	Cheesy Broccoli Chicken	Shrimp & Mushrooms	Mixed Berries Cheesecake Fat Bomb

7	Fennel Brown Hash	Creamy Scallops	Sesame Pork and Bean Sprout	Cinnamon Swirl Bread
8	Parmesan Omelette	Parmesan Beef Roast	Salmon Boards	Peanut Fat Bombs
9	Strawberries & Cream	Cod Quesadillas	Beef Burger with Sriracha Mayo	Blackberry Shake
10	Coconut Pancakes	Parmesan Baked Turkey	Buttery Garlic Turkey	Cocoa Fat bomb
11	Parmesan Egg Muffins	Turkey Skewers with Peanut Sauce	Steak Bibimbap	Cinnamon Swirl Bread
12	English Scrambled Eggs	Parmesan Beef Roast	Shrimp & Mushrooms	Peanut Fat Bombs

13	Parmesan Omelette	Snapper Taco Bowl	Juicy Barbecue Ribs	Mixed Berries Cheesecake Fat Bomb
14	Egg Filled Avocado	Creamy Scallops	Salmon Boards	Blackberry Shake
15	Strawberries & Cream	Parmesan Baked Turkey	Keto Tuna Pie	Almond Fat Bombs
16	Fennel Brown Hash	Cheesy Broccoli Chicken	Juicy Barbecue Ribs	Root Beer Float
17	English Scrambled Eggs	Cod Quesadillas	Shrimp & Mushrooms	Cinnamon Swirl Bread
18	Almond Pancakes	Turkey Skewers with Peanut Sauce	Steak Bibimbap	Cocoa Fat Bomb
19	Egg Filled Avocado	Parmesan Beef Roast	Salmon Boards	Mixed Berries Cheesecake Fat Bomb

20	Parmesan Omelette	Snapper Taco Bowl	Buttery Garlic Turkey	Blackberry Shake
21	English Scrambled Eggs	Creamy Scallops	Shrimp & Mushrooms	Root Beer Float

Now that you know the plan for the next 21 days, let's track your goals and successes.

Success Journal

Documenting your achievements in the first few days of your keto journey can help create lifelong trends and help you catapult your body into ketosis. The next few pages will offer you a safe space to journal for the first 21 days.

Let's begin! Take a breath. You got this!

Keto Goals

What are the goals you would like to achieve in the first 21 days of your keto journey?

1. _____

2. _____

3. _____

4. _____

5. _____

6. _____

7. _____

8. _____

9. _____

10. _____

11. _____

12. _____

13. _____

14. _____

15. _____

16. _____

17. _____

18. _____

19. _____

20. _____

21. _____

Were You Successful in These Goals?

Tracking goal fulfilment not only helps you to gain confidence in your journey but also helps you identify points in which you need to work on.

Shade in the circle for each day you were successful., You will need to recreate this chart in your journal.

Week 1 Day 1 | Day 2 | Day 3 | Day 4 | Day 5 | Day 6 | Day 7

Week 2 Day 8 | Day 9 | Day 10 | Day 11 | Day 12 | Day 13 | Day 14

Week 3 Day 15 | Day 16 | Day 17 | Day 18 | Day 19 | Day 20 | Day 21

What Was Your Starting Point?

Let's get your starting measurements and weight., You will need to recreate this chart in your journal.

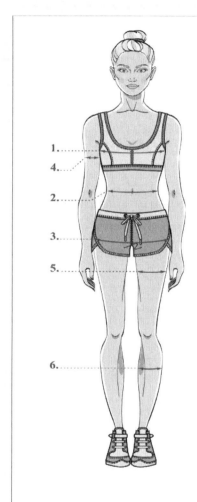

1. Bust: _____

2. Waist: _____

3. Hips: _____

4. Biceps: _____

5. Thighs: _____

6. Calf: _____

7. Weight _____

What Were Your Results?

Now that you have utilized the 21-day action plan, what are your ending measurements and weight on day 22? You will need to recreate this chart in your journal.

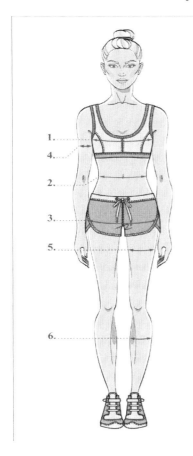

1. Bust: _____

2. Waist: _____

3. Hips: _____

4. Biceps: _____

5. Thighs: _____

6. Calf: _____

7. Weight _____

Congrats on completing your first 21 days! Now that you've got into the swing of things, let's explore a few more delicious recipes to help keep you on track.

Measurement Conversions

It is important to note that it is virtually impossible to include an all-inclusive conversion table as all foods have slightly different measurements when converted.

KITCHEN CONVERSIONS

LIQUID CONVERSIONS

1/4 TSP	=	1 ML				
1/2 TSP	=	2 ML				
1 TSP	=	5 ML				
3 TSP	=	1 TBL	= 1/2 FL OZ	= 15 ML		
2 TBLS	=	1/8 CUP	= 1 FL OZ	= 30 ML		
4 TBLS	=	1/4 CUP	= 2 FL OZ	= 60 ML		
5 1/3 TBLS	=	1/3 CUP	= 3 FL OZ	= 80 ML		
8 TBLS	=	1/2 CUP	= 4 FL OZ	= 120 ML		
10 2/3	=	2/3 CUP	= 5 FL OZ	= 160 ML		
12 TBLS	=	3/4 CUP	= 6 FL OZ	= 180 ML		
16 TBLS	=	1 CUP	= 8 FL OZ	= 240 ML		
1 PT	=	2 CUPS	= 16 FL OZ	= 480 ML		
1 QT	=	4 CUPS	= 32 FL OZ	= 960 ML		
33 FL OZ	=	1000 ML	= 1 L			

Length

METRIC	IMPERIAL
3mm	1/8 inch
6mm	1/4 inch
2.5cm	1 inch
3cm	1 1/4 inch
5cm	2 inches
10cm	4 inches
15cm	6 inches
20cm	8 inches
22.5cm	9 inches
25cm	10 inches
28cm	11 inches

Oven Temperatures

	Fahrenheit	Celsius	Gas Mark
Freezing Water	32°F	0°C	
Room Temp.	68°F	20°C	
Boiling Water	212° F	100°C	
Baking	325° F	160°C	3
	350° F	180°C	4
	375° F	190°C	5
	400° F	200°C	6
	425° F	220°C	7
	450° F	230°C	8
Broiling			Grill

Weight Conversions

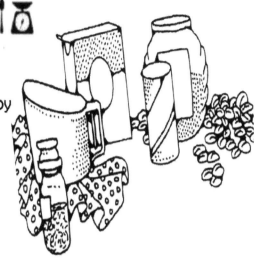

(To convert ounces to grams, multiply the number of ounces by 30.)

1 oz	=	1/16 lb	=	30 g
4 oz	=	1/4 lb	=	120 g
8 oz	=	1/2 lb	=	240 g
12 oz	=	3/4 lb	=	360 g
16 oz	=	1 lb	=	480 g

Conversions for Different Types of Food

Standard Cup	Fine Powder (like flour)	Grains (like rice)	Granular (like sugar)	Liquid Solids (like butter)	Liquid (eg. milk)
1	140 g	150 g	190 g	200 g	240 ml
3/4	105 g	113 g	143 g	150 g	180 ml
2/3	93 g	100 g	125 g	133 g	160 ml
1/2	70 g	75 g	95 g	100 g	120 ml
1/3	47 g	50 g	63 g	67 g	80 ml
1/4	35 g	38 g	48 g	50 g	60 ml
1/8	18 g	19 g	24 g	25 g	30 ml

Breakfast

English Scrambled Eggs

Serves: 4
Prep Time: 5 mins
Cook Time: 10 mins

Ingredients:

- 6 large eggs, lightly beaten
- 2 Jalapeños, pickled, chopped finely
- 1 Tomato, diced
- 85 g Cheese, shredded
- 2 tbsp. Butter, for frying
- 35ml Full Cream Milk

Directions:

1. Set a large skillet with butter over medium heat and allow to melt.
2. Add tomatoes, jalapeños and green onions then cook, while stirring, until fragrant, about 3 minutes.
3. Whisk together the egg and full cream then add the egg mixture, and continue to cook, while stirring, until almost set, about 2 minutes. Add cheese, and season to taste.
4. Continue cooking until the cheese melts, about another minute. Serve, and enjoy.

Calories: 239   Carbs: 2.38g   Protein: 13.92g   Fats: 19.32g

Spinach Quiche

Serves: 4
Prep Time: 15 mins
Cook Time:18 mins

Ingredients:

- ❖ 170g Celery stalk, chopped
- ❖ 130g Spinach
- ❖ 5 Eggs
- ❖ 65g Almond flour
- ❖ 1 teaspoon Olive oil
- ❖ 1 tablespoon Butter
- ❖ 1 teaspoon Salt
- ❖ 30g Double cream,
- ❖ 1 teaspoon Ground black pepper

Directions:

1. Chop the spinach and combine it with the chopped celery stalk in the big bowl.
2. Beat the egg in the separate bowl and whisk them.
3. Combine the whisked eggs with the almond flour, butter, salt, double cream, and ground black pepper. Whisk it.
4. Preheat the air fryer to 190 degrees C.
5. Spray the air fryer basket tray with the olive oil inside.
6. Then add the spinach-fennel mixture and pour the whisked egg mixture.
7. Cook the quiche for 18 minutes. When the time is over – let the quiche chill little.
8. Then remove it from the air fryer and slice into the servings. Enjoy!

Calories: 249   Carbs: 9.4g   Protein: 11.3g   Fats: 19.1g

Parmesan Egg Muffins

Serves: 6
Prep Time: 10 mins
Cook Time: 20 mins

Ingredients:
- ❖ 4 large Eggs
- ❖ 2 tbsp. Greek yogurt, full fat
- ❖ 3 tbsp. Almond flour
- ❖ ¼ tsp. Baking powder
- ❖ 190g Parmesan cheese, shredded

Directions:
1. Set your oven to preheat to 200 degrees C.
2. Add yogurt, and eggs to a medium bowl, season with salt, and pepper, then whisk to combine. Add your baking powder, and flour, then mix to form a smooth batter.
3. Finally, add your cheese, and fold to combine. Pour your mixture evenly into 6 silicone muffin cups and set to bake in your preheated oven.
4. Allow to bake until your eggs are fully set, and lightly golden on top, about 20 minutes, turning the tray at the halfway point.
5. Allow muffins to cool on a cooling rack then serve. Enjoy!

Calories: 144   Carbs: 1.43g   Protein: 8.02g   Fats: 11.9g

Coconut Flour Bok Choy Casserole

Serves: 6
Prep Time: 30 mins
Cook Time: 30 mins

Ingredients:

- ❖ 8 Eggs
- ❖ 100g Unsweetened almond milk
- ❖ 140g Fresh spinach, chopped
- ❖ 170g Bok choy, chopped
- ❖ 130g Parmesan, grated
- ❖ 3 Minced Garlic cloves
- ❖ 1 tsp Salt
- ❖ ½ tsp Pepper
- ❖ 100g Coconut flour
- ❖ 1 tbsp Baking powder

Directions:

1. Preheat your air fryer to a temperature of about 190° C. Grease your air fryer pan with cooking spray.
2. Whisk the eggs with the almond milk, the spinach, the bok choy, parmesan cheese. Add the garlic, the salt and the pepper.
3. Add the coconut flour and baking powder and whisk until very well combined.
4. Spread mixture into your air fryer pan and sprinkle the remaining quantity of cheese over it.
5. Place the baking pan in the air fryer and lock the air fryer and set the timer to about 30 minutes.
6. When the timer beeps; turn off your Air Fryer. Remove the baking pan from the air fryer and sprinkle with the chopped basil. Slice your dish; then serve and enjoy it!

Calories: 175.6   Carbs: 2.4g   Protein: 17.7g   Fats: 10.3g

Parmesan Omelette

Serves: 2
Prep Time: 10 mins
Cook Time: 10 mins

Ingredients:

- ❖ 6 Eggs, beaten
- ❖ 2 tbsp. Olive oil
- ❖ 100g Tomatoes, cherry, halved
- ❖ 1 tbsp. Basil, dried
- ❖ 165g Parmesan cheese, diced

Directions:

1. Whisk basil into eggs, and lightly season.
2. Set a large skillet with oil over medium heat and allow to get hot. Once hot, add tomatoes and cook while stirring.
3. Top with egg and continue cooking until the tops have started to firm up.
4. Add cheese, switch your heat to low, and allow to set fully set before serving. Enjoy!

Calories: 423   Carbs: 6.81g   Protein: 43.08g   Fats: 60.44g

Egg Filled Avocado

Serves: 4
Prep Time: 15 mins
Cook Time: 15 mins

Ingredients:

- ❖ 3 Halved Avocados
- ❖ 6 Eggs
- ❖ 1 tsp Garlic powder
- ❖ ½ tsp Sea salt
- ❖ ¼ tsp Black pepper
- ❖ 30g Parmesan cheese, shredded

Directions:

1. Preheat your air fryer at a temperature of about 190 °C.
2. Take 3 medium avocados; then cut it into halves. Scoop out about one third of the meat from each of the avocados.
3. Put the avocado halves in the air fryer pan with the face up.
4. Sprinkle the avocado with 1 pinch of salt and 1 pinch of pepper.
5. Sprinkle with the garlic powder and crack each of the eggs in the avocado halves.
6. Place the Air Fryer pan in your air fryer basket and lock the lid.
7. Set the timer for about 13 to 15 minutes.
8. When the timer beeps; turn off your Air Fryer.
9. Serve and enjoy your breakfast!

Calories: 223   Carbs: 4g   Protein: 8g   Fats: 12.6g

Almond Pancakes

Serves: 4
Prep Time: 5 mins
Cook Time: 20 mins

Ingredients:

- ❖ 4 Eggs
- ❖ 170g Cottage cheese
- ❖ 1 tbsp. Almond Flour
- ❖ 60g Butter

Directions:

1. Add all your ingredients except butter, to a medium bowl, stir to combine then set aside to expand for about 5 minutes.
2. Set a skillet with oil over medium heat and allow to melt.
3. Add batter to the hot pan in batches and allow to fry until lightly golden on each side, about 4 minutes per side.
4. Serve with berries or whipped cream.

Calories: 302   Carbs: 2.69g   Protein: 14.52g   Fats: 25.87g

Strawberries & Cream

Serves: 1
Prep Time: 2 mins
Cook Time: 0 mins

Ingredients:
- ❖ 70g Coconut cream
- ❖ 65g Strawberries
- ❖ 1 tsp. Vanilla extract

Directions:
1. Add coconut cream, and vanilla Ingredients to a blender then process until thick and smooth.
2. Transfer to a serving bowl, top with strawberries, and serve.

Calories: 426   Carbs: 12.87g   Protein: 4.74g   Fats: 41.79g

Fennel Brown Hash

Serves: 2
Prep Time: 10 mins
Cook Time: 20 mins

Ingredients:

- 1 small onion, sliced
- 6 to 8 medium Mushrooms, sliced
- 260g Ground beef
- 1 Pinch Salt
- 1 Pinch Ground black pepper
- ½ tsp Smoked paprika
- 2 Eggs, lightly beaten
- 1 Small Avocado, diced
- 170g Fennel, chopped

Directions:

1. Preheat your air fryer to a temperature of about 190° C.
2. Spray your air fryer pan with a little bit of melted coconut oil.
3. Add the onions, the mushrooms, the salt and the pepper to the pan.
4. Add in the ground beef, smoked paprika and fennel. Crack in the eggs.
5. Gently whisk your mixture; then place the pan in your Air Fryer and lock the lid.
6. Set the timer to about 18 to 20 minutes and the temperature to about 200° C.
7. When the timer beeps; turn off your Air Fryer; then remove the pan from the Air Fryer.
8. Serve and enjoy your breakfast with chopped parsley and diced avocado!

Calories: 290   **Carbs: 15g**   **Protein: 20g**   **Fats: 23g**

Almond Crepes

Serves: 2
Prep Time: 5 mins
Cook Time: 10 mins

Ingredients:

- 4 Eggs
- 30g Almond milk, unsweetened
- 1 tbsp. Almond flour
- 30g Parsley, finely chopped
- 2 tbsp. Coconut oil, for frying

Directions:

1. Combine all your crepe ingredients into a medium bowl, then whisk until a smooth batter is formed.
2. Allow the mixture to stand like this for about 10 minutes to thicken a little.
3. Set a large, greased skillet over medium heat to get hot.
4. Stir the batter and add a few tablespoons of the batter to the center of your hot skillet.
5. Swirl the skillet so that the batter spreads and creates a thin layer over the bottom of the skillet.
6. Allow to cook for about 2 minutes, or until golden brown. Transfer from heat to a serving plate and serve.

Calories: 263   Carbs: 3.05g   Protein: 12.24g   Fats: 22.73g

Coconut Pancakes

Serves: 2-3
Prep Time: 5 mins
Cook Time: 5 mins

Ingredients:
- ❖ 2 Separated large Eggs
- ❖ 55g of heavy whipping cream
- ❖ 2 tsp granulated erythritol
- ❖ 1 Pinch sea salt
- ❖ 65g finely ground coconut flour
- ❖ ¼ tsp gluten free baking powder
- ❖ 1 tsp of unsalted butter

Directions:
1. Combine the whipping cream with the egg yolks, the low carb sweetener and the salt; mix very well until your mixture becomes smooth.
2. In a bowl; mix the coconut flour with the baking powder and add it to the mixture of egg and mix very well.
3. Plug your air fryer into power; then spray the baking pan of your air fryer with cooking spray.
4. Pour the batter in your pan and spread it very well with the back of a spoon.
5. Place the baking dish in the basket of your air fryer and close the lid.
6. Set the temperature to about 200° C and set the timer for about 5 minutes.
7. When the timer beeps, unplug your air fryer. Serve and enjoy your pancakes!

Calories: 330   **Carbs: 7g**   **Protein: 12g**   **Fats: 29g**

Cinnamon French Toast

Serves: 2
Prep Time: 6 mins
Cook Time: 8 mins

Ingredients:

- 4 Large pieces of cinnamon swirl bread (recipe below)
- 2 Tbsp margarine
- 2 Beaten eggs
- 1 Pinch of salt
- 1 tsp nutmeg
- A few ground cloves

Directions:

1. Preheat your Air fryer to a temperature of about 180°C.
2. In a large bowl, beat the eggs, 1 sprinkle of salt, and small pinch of nutmeg.
3. Add the ground cloves and butter both the sides of the bread; then cut the bread into strips.
4. Dredge each of the bread strips into the mixture of eggs and arrange it into your Air Fryer.
5. After about 2 minutes of cooking, pause your Air fryer, then remove the pan and place it over a heat safe place.
6. Spray the bread with cooking spray on both sides; then return the bread strips to the pan and place it again in your air fryer.
7. Cook the bread slices for about 4 minutes and make sure to check after each 2-minute interval to avoid burning.
8. When the timer beeps; turn off your Air Fryer. Serve and enjoy your breakfast!

Calories: 300   Carbs: 4.4g   Protein: 14g   Fats: 76g

Spinach, Salmon & Eggs

Serves: 1
Prep Time: 10 mins.
Cook Time: 15 mins.

Ingredients:
- ❖ 2 tbsp double cream
- ❖ 1 tbsp butter
- ❖ 28g baby spinach
- ❖ 2 eggs
- ❖ 55g smoked salmon
- ❖ Salt and pepper for seasoning

Directions:
1. Take a large frying pan and add the butter over a medium heat.
2. Add the spinach and allow to soften.
3. Add the cream and stir, waiting for it to bubble.
4. Crack the eggs into the pan and mix everything until combined.
5. Season to your liking.
6. Stir and cook until the eggs are as you like them.
7. Arrange the scrambled eggs on your serving plate with the smoked salmon the side.

Calories: 419   Carbs: 2 g   Protein: 25g   Fats: 34g

Breakfast Broth

Serves: 4
Prep Time: 10 mins.
Cook Time: 8-24 hrs. 20 mins.

Ingredients:
- 2.3kg beef bones
- 1 chopped onion
- 1 chopped carrot
- 1 crushed garlic clove
- 3 tbsp coconut oil, melted
- 1 tbsp white wine vinegar
- 1 tbsp salt
- 1 tbsp pepper
- Water

Directions:
1. Preheat your oven to 225 degrees C.
2. Take a large baking dish and arrange the bones inside.
3. Take the melted oil and brush the bones carefully.
4. Place the dish in the oven and cook for around 15. Hours, until the bones are brown. You may need to turn them over halfway through, depending on how you've arranged them.
5. Towards the end of the cooking time, add up to 250ml of water, to stop the juices burning in the bottom of the dish.
6. Once cooked, place the bones into a large cooking pot.
7. Add enough water to cover the top of the bones with a few inches left to spare.
8. Cook over a medium heat, allowing to boil for up to 15 minutes.
9. Reduce the heat and allow to simmer for anything between 8 to 24 hours, depending upon when you want to eat the broth!
10. Once cooked, strain the mixture using a cheesecloth or a mesh and allow to cool a little.

Calories: 134   Carbs: 0.03g   Protein: 4g   Fats: 13g

Healthy Breakfast Wraps

Serves: 2
Prep Time: 15 mins.
Cook Time: 15 mins.

Ingredients:

- ❖ 3 tbsp mayonnaise
- ❖ 170g bacon
- ❖ 55g lettuce
- ❖ 1 sliced tomato
- ❖ Half a sliced avocado
- ❖ Salt and pepper for seasoning

Directions:

1. Take a large skillet pan and add the bacon, frying until crisp.
2. Place the bacon on a paper towel and blot.
3. Cut the bacon into slices.
4. Arrange the lettuce leaves individually.
5. Place a line of squeeze mayonnaise onto each lettuce leaf.
6. Add a slice of tomato onto each lettuce lave.
7. Add three slices of bacon onto each lettuce leaf.
8. Add a slice of avocado onto each lettuce leave.
9. Season before serving.

Calories: 631   Carbs: 4 g   Protein: 31g   Fats: 53g

Classic Egg Breakfast

Serves: 1
Prep Time: 10 mins.
Cook Time: 3-4 mins.

Ingredients:

- 0.5 tbsp olive oil
- 1 tbsp mayonnaise
- 2 eggs
- 28g baby spinach
- Salt and pepper for seasoning

Directions:

1. Take a medium frying pan and add the oil over medium heat.
2. Crack the eggs into the pan and fry to your liking
3. Serve the eggs with the spinach on the side and a small amount of mayonnaise
4. Season to your liking

Calories: 297   Carbs: 1g   Protein: 14g   Fats: 26g

Cheesy Waffles

Serves: 4
Prep Time: 10 mins.
Cook Time: 15 mins.

Ingredients:
- ❖ 4 eggs
- ❖ 4 tbsp almond flour
- ❖ 220g shredded mozzarella cheese
- ❖ 28g melted butter
- ❖ Salt and pepper for seasoning

Directions:
1. For this recipe you will need a waffle maker. Grease the waffle maker and preheat.
2. Take a large mixing bowl and add all the ingredients, combining well.
3. Add an even layer of the mixture into your waffle maker and ensure it is distributed throughout.
4. Close the waffle machine and cook for 6 minutes.
5. Remove once slightly crispy and brown, and repeat to create another batch.

Calories: 331   **Carbs: 2 g**   **Protein: 20g**   **Fats: 27g**

Onion & Bacon Breakfast Pancake

Serves: 4
Prep Time: 10 mins.
Cook Time: 15 mins.

Ingredients:

- 100g bacon
- 2 tbsp butter
- Half a chopped onion
- 4 eggs
- 240ml double cream
- 120ml cottage cheese
- 1 tsp baking powder
- 1 tbsp ground psyllium powder
- 120ml almond flour
- Salt and pepper for seasoning

Directions:

1. Preheat your oven to 190 degrees C.
2. Cut the onion into small pieces.
3. Take a large frying pan and add the butter over a medium heat.
4. Cook the onion and bacon for a few minutes.
5. Take a mixing bowl and add the cottage cheese, cream, and eggs, combining well with a whisk.
6. Add the rest of the ingredients and combine once more.
7. Allow the mixture to sit for a few minutes.
8. Take a medium sized oven dish and grease well.
9. Pour the mixture into the pan and ensure it is evenly distributed.
10. Add the onion and bacon over the top.
11. Place in the oven and bake for 20 minutes, until fully cooked through.

Calories: 553   **Carbs: 5 g**   **Protein: 22g**   **Fats: 49g**

Devilled Eggs, Keto-Style

Serves: 4
Prep Time: 15 mins.
Cook Time: 10 mins.

Ingredients:

- 60ml mayonnaise
- 1 tsp tabasco sauce
- 16 shrimps, cooked and peeled
- 8 eggs
- Salt and pepper to season
- A few dill sprigs (fresh)

Directions:

1. Take a large saucepan and add the eggs.
2. Cover with water, so the eggs are covered by about 5cm of water.
3. Cover the pan over and bring to the boil.
4. Once the pan starts to boil, turn the heat off and let the eggs sit for 10 minutes.
5. Take a slotted spoon and remove the eggs, placing them in a bath of ice. Wait for a few minutes before you peel away the shells.
6. Cut the eggs in half and remove the yolks with a spoon.
7. Arrange the egg whites on your serving place.
8. Take a medium mixing bowl and add the yolks, mashing them down with a fork.
9. Add the tabasco, mayonnaise, and seasoning, combining well.
10. Add a little of the mixture to each egg white and then top each one with a shrimp.
11. Sprinkle with a little chopped dill and serve.

Calories: 230   Carbs: 1 g   Protein: 13g   Fats: 19g

Scrambled Feta & Spinach

Serves: 2
Prep Time: 10 mins.
Cook Time: 8 mins.

Ingredients:

- ❖ 1 tbsp double cream
- ❖ 1 tbsp butter
- ❖ 4 eggs
- ❖ 45g crumbled feta cheese
- ❖ 1 minced garlic clove
- ❖ 85g bacon
- ❖ 110g baby spinach, fresh
- ❖ Salt and pepper for seasoning

Directions:

1. Take a medium mixing bowl and add the cream and eggs, whisking until combined.
2. Take a large skillet pan and add the butter, heating over a medium heat.
3. Add the garlic and spinach and cook for a few minutes, until the spinach has wilted.
4. Season and combine again.
5. Pour the mixture into the pan and allow the edges to set.
6. Use a spatula to carefully lift the edges and allowing the uncooked egg to move and cook.
7. Cook until the eggs are cooked to your preference.
8. Remove the omelette from the pan and place on a serving plate.
9. Sprinkle the cheese over the top and add a few slices of bacon on the side.

Calories: 491   **Carbs: 4g**   **Protein: 32g**   **Fats: 38g**

Cheesy Breakfast Omelette

Serves: 2
Prep Time: 10 mins.
Cook Time: 8 mins.

Ingredients:
- ❖ 85g butter
- ❖ 200g grated cheese
- ❖ 6 eggs
- ❖ Salt and pepper for seasoning

Directions:
1. Crack the eggs into a mixing bowl and whisk well.
2. Add half of the cheese, season and combine once more.
3. Take a medium frying pan and add the butter over a medium heat, until melted.
4. Add the mixture into the pan and cook for two minutes, until starting to firm.
5. Turn the heat down a little and add the rest of the cheese.
6. Fold and cook for 1 more minute, before serving.

Calories: 895   Carbs: 4 g   Protein: 40g   Fats: 80g

Avocado Eggs Benedict

Serves: 4
Prep Time: 10 mins.
Cook Time: 12 mins.

Ingredients:

- ❖ 100g butter
- ❖ 3 egg yolks
- ❖ 1 tbsp lemon juice
- ❖ 4 large eggs
- ❖ 140g smoked salmon

- ❖ 2 pitted and skinned avocados, stone removed and cut into halves
- ❖ Salt and pepper for seasoning

Directions:

1. Take a microwave safe jar and add the butter, placing in the microwave to melt for a few seconds.
2. Add the lemon juice and the yolks.
3. Take an immersion blender and blend until the mixture turns creamy and almost white.
4. Season to your liking.
5. Take a medium saucepan and add water, bringing it to the boil.
6. Once boiling, reduce the temperature to medium-low.
7. Take a measuring cup and crack one egg inside, carefully sliding it into the boiling water.
8. Repeat for the other eggs.
9. Cook for 3 or 4 minutes, depending on how you like your eggs.
10. Remove them with a slotted spoon and allow them to sit on paper towels for a minute.

11. Arrange the avocados on the serving plate and slice the bottom of each one so it sits and doesn't topple over.
12. Add an egg on top of each slice of avocado.
13. Add a spoon of the sauce on top.
14. Arrange some smoked salmon at the side.
15. Eat immediately.

Calories: 255   **Carbs: 5 g**   **Protein: 44g**   **Fats: 75g**

Lunch

Snapper Taco Bowl

Serves: 2
Prep Time: 10 mins
Cook Time: 15 mins.

Ingredients:

- 260g snapper fillets
- 24g Tajin seasoning salt, divided
- 340g pre-sliced coleslaw cabbage mix
- 14g Spicy Red Pepper Miso Mayo,
- 1 avocado, mashed

Directions:

1. Set your oven to preheat to 220 degrees C. Line a baking sheet with aluminum foil or a silicone baking mat.
2. Rub the snapper with the olive oil, and then coat it with 2 teaspoons of Tajin seasoning salt. Place the fish in the prepared pan.
3. Bake for 15 minutes, or until the fish is opaque when you pierce it with a fork.
4. Put the fish on a cooling rack and let it sit for 4 minutes.
5. Meanwhile, in a medium bowl, gently mix to combine the coleslaw and the mayo sauce.
6. Add the mashed avocado and the remaining 2 teaspoons of Tajin seasoning salt to the coleslaw, and season with pink salt and pepper. Divide the salad between two bowls.
7. Use two forks to shred the fish into small pieces and add it to the bowls.
8. Top the fish with a drizzle of mayo sauce and serve.

Calories: 315   Carbs: 12g   Protein: 16g   Fats: 24g

Cod Quesadilla

Serves: 2
Prep Time: 5 mins
Cook Time: 5 mins.

Ingredients:
- ❖ 15 ml olive oil
- ❖ 2 low-carbohydrate tortillas
- ❖ 55g shredded Mexican blend cheese
- ❖ 100g shredded cod
- ❖ 30g sour cream

Directions:
1. In a large skillet over medium-high heat, heat the olive oil.
2. Add a tortilla, then layer with half of cheese, the cod, the Tajin seasoning, and the remaining cheese. Top with the second tortilla.
3. Peek under the edge of the bottom tortilla to monitor how it is browning.
4. Once the bottom tortilla gets golden, and the cheese begins to melt, after about 2 minutes, flip the quesadilla over, and cook for about a minute.
5. Once the second tortilla is crispy and golden, transfer the quesadilla to a cutting board and let sit for 2 minutes. Cut the quesadilla into 4 wedges using a sharp knife.
6. Transfer half the quesadilla to each of two plates. Add a tablespoon of sour cream to each plate and serve hot.

Calories: 312   Carbs: 19g   Protein: 26g   Fats: 28g

Baked Lemon-Butter Sea Bass

Serves: 2
Prep Time: 10 mins
Cook Time: 20 mins.

Ingredients:
- ❖ 4 tablespoons butter, plus more for coating
- ❖ 2 150g Sea Bass fillets
- ❖ 2 garlic cloves, minced
- ❖ 1 lemon, zested and juiced
- ❖ 2 tablespoons capers, rinsed and chopped

Directions:
1. Set oven to preheat to 200 degrees C. Coat an 8-inch baking dish with butter.
2. Pat dry the Sea Bass with paper towels, and season both sides to taste. Place in the prepared baking dish.
3. In a medium skillet over medium heat, melt the butter. Add the garlic and cook for 3 to 5 minutes, until slightly browned but not burned.
4. Remove the garlic butter from the heat and mix in the lemon zest and 2 tablespoons of lemon juice.
5. Pour the lemon-butter sauce over the fish and sprinkle the capers around the baking pan.
6. Bake for 12 to 15 minutes, until the fish, is just cooked through, and serve.

Calories: 299   **Carbs: 5g**   **Protein: 16g**   **Fats: 26g**

Creamy Scallops

Serves: 2
Prep Time: 5 mins
Cook Time: 20 mins.

Ingredients:
- ❖ 4 turkey bacon slices
- ❖ 260ml whipping cream
- ❖ 40g grated Parmesan cheese
- ❖ 1 tablespoon ghee
- ❖ 8 large sea scallops, rinsed and patted dry

Directions:
1. In a medium skillet over medium-high heat, allow your turkey bacon to cook until crisp, about 8 minutes. Drain turkey bacon on a plate will paper towels.
2. Lower the heat to medium. Keep your turkey bacon grease then add cream, butter, and Parmesan cheese.
3. Season to taste then reduce the heat to low and cook, stirring constantly, until the sauce thickens and is reduced by 50 percent, about 10 minutes.
4. In a separate large skillet over medium-high heat, heat the ghee until sizzling.
5. Season the scallops with pink salt and pepper and add them to the skillet. Cook for just 1 minute per side.
6. Transfer the scallops to a paper towel–lined plate. Divide the cream sauce between two plates, crumble the turkey bacon on top of the cream sauce, and top with 4 scallops each. Serve immediately.

Calories: 782   **Carbs: 11g**   **Protein: 24g**   **Fats: 73g**

Garlic-Parmesan Chicken Wings

Serves: 2
Prep Time: 10 mins
Cook Time: 3 hrs.

Ingredients:
- ❖ 1 kg Chicken Wings.
- ❖ Garlic, 4 cloves, chopped
- ❖ 60g Coconut Aminos
- ❖ 1 tbsp. Fish Sauce
- ❖ 2 tbsp. Sesame Oil

Directions:
1. Put wings into a large bowl, drain or pat to dry.
2. In a small saucepan heat your ingredients, except wings. Remove from flame and add sesame oil.
3. Pour mixture over wings and stir. Cool and refrigerate overnight, you may stir occasionally as it marinates.
4. Remove wings from marinade and bake wings at 180 degrees C until they are done.
5. Remove from heat and enjoy. Add your favorite side dish or have as is.

Calories: 738   Carbs: 4g   Protein: 39g   Fats: 66g

Turkey Skewers with Peanut Sauce

Serves: 2
Prep Time: 1hr. 10 mins.
Cook Time: 15 mins.

Ingredients:

- 500g boneless skinless turkey breast cut into chunks
- 3 tablespoons soy sauce divided
- ½ teaspoon Sriracha sauce, plus ¼ teaspoon
- 3 teaspoons toasted sesame oil, divided
- 2 tablespoons peanut butter

Directions:

1. In a large zip-top bag, combine the turkey chunks with 2 tablespoons of soy sauce, ½ teaspoon of Sriracha sauce, and 2 teaspoons of sesame oil.
2. Seal the bag, and let the turkey marinate for an hour or so in the refrigerator or up to overnight.
3. If you are using wood 8-inch skewers, soak them in water for 30 minutes before using.
4. I like to use my grill pan for the skewers because I don't have an outdoor grill. If you don't have a grill pan, you can use a large skillet. Preheat your grill pan or grill to low. Oil the grill pan with ghee.
5. Thread the turkey chunks onto the skewers.
6. Cook the skewers over low heat for 10 to 15 minutes, flipping halfway through.
7. Meanwhile, mix the peanut dipping sauce. Stir together the remaining 1 tablespoon of soy sauce, ¼ teaspoon of Sriracha sauce, 1 teaspoon of sesame oil, and the peanut butter. Season with pink salt and pepper.
8. Serve the turkey skewers with a small dish of the peanut sauce.

Calories: 586   Carbs: 15g   Protein: 75g   Fats: 29g

Parmesan Baked Turkey

Serves: 2
Prep Time: 5 mins.
Cook Time: 20 mins.

Ingredients:

- 2 tablespoons ghee
- 2 boneless skinless turkey breasts
- 230g mayonnaise
- 80g grated Parmesan cheese
- 60g crushed pork rinds

Directions:

1. Preheat the oven to 220°C. Choose a baking dish that is large enough to hold both turkey breasts and coat it with the ghee.
2. Pat dry the turkey breasts with a paper towel, season with pink salt and pepper, and place in the prepared baking dish.
3. In a small bowl, mix to combine the mayonnaise, Parmesan cheese, and Italian seasoning.
4. Slather the mayonnaise mixture evenly over the turkey breasts and sprinkle the crushed pork rinds on top of the mayonnaise mixture.
5. Bake until the topping is browned, about 20 minutes, and serve.

Calories: 850   **Carbs: 2g**   **Protein: 60g**   **Fats: 67g**

Cheesy Broccoli Chicken

Serves: 2
Prep Time: 10 mins.
Cook Time: 1 hour

Ingredients:
- 2 boneless skinless chicken breasts
- 4 bacon slices
- 170 cream cheese, room temp.
- 350g frozen broccoli florets thawed
- 50g shredded Cheddar cheese

Directions:
1. Set your oven to preheat to 200 degrees C.
2. Choose a baking dish that is large enough to hold both chicken breasts and coat it with the ghee.
3. Pat dry the chicken breasts with a paper towel, and season with pink salt and pepper.
4. Place the chicken breasts and the bacon slices in the baking dish and bake for 25 minutes.
5. Transfer the chicken to a cutting board and use two forks to shred it. Season it again with pink salt and pepper.
6. Place the bacon on a paper towel–lined plate to crisp up, and then crumble it.
7. In a medium bowl, mix to combine the cream cheese, shredded chicken, broccoli, and half of the bacon crumbles.
8. Transfer the chicken mixture to the baking dish, and top with the Cheddar and the remaining half of the bacon crumbles.
9. Bake until the cheese is bubbling and browned about 35 minutes and serve.

Calories: 935   **Carbs: 10g**   **Protein: 75g**   **Fats: 66g**

Parmesan Beef Roast

Serves: 2
Prep Time: 10 mins.
Cook Time: 25 mins.

Ingredients:
- ❖ 30g grated Parmesan cheese
- ❖ 2 boneless beef roasts
- ❖ Olive oil, for drizzling
- ❖ 250g asparagus spears, tough ends snapped off

Directions:
1. Set oven to preheat to 190 degrees C and prepare a baking sheet by lining it with foil.
2. In a medium bowl, mix to combine the Parmesan cheese, and garlic powder.
3. Pat the beef roasts dry with a paper towel, and season to taste.
4. Place a beef roast in the bowl with the Parmesan–pork rind mixture and press the "breading" to the beef roast, so it sticks.
5. Place the coated beef roast on the prepared baking sheet. Repeat for the second beef roast.
6. Drizzle a small amount of olive oil over each beef roast.
7. Place the asparagus on the baking sheet around the beef roasts.
8. Drizzle with olive oil, and season to taste. Sprinkle any leftover Parmesan cheese–pork rind mixture over the asparagus.
9. Bake for 20 to 25 minutes. Thinner beef roasts will cook faster than thicker ones.
10. Serve hot.

Calories: 370   **Carbs: 6g**   **Protein: 40g**   **Fats: 21g**

Slow Cooker Pork Roast

Serves: 4
Prep Time: 10 mins.
Cook Time: 8 hrs.

Ingredients:
- ❖ 1kg Pork chuck roast
- ❖ 4 chipotle peppers in adobo sauce
- ❖ can green jalapeño chilis
- ❖ 2 tablespoons apple cider vinegar
- ❖ 100ml Pork broth

Directions:
1. With the crock insert in place, preheat your slow cooker to low.
2. Season the Pork chuck roast on both sides with pink salt and pepper. Put the roast in your slow cooker.
3. In a food processor, or blender, combine the chipotle peppers and their adobo sauce, jalapeños, and apple cider vinegar, and pulse until smooth. Add the Pork broth and pulse a few more times. Pour the chili mixture over the top of the roast.
4. Cover and cook on low for 8 hours.
5. Transfer the Pork to a cutting board and use two forks to shred the meat.
6. Serve hot.

Calories: 723   **Carbs: 7g**   **Protein: 66g**   **Fats: 46g**

Mini Keto Meatloaves

Serves: 8
Prep Time: 20 mins.
Cook Time: 40 minutes

Ingredients:

- ❖ 500g. of 85% lean ground Beef
- ❖ ¾ of a teaspoon of kosher salt
- ❖ ¼ of a teaspoon of black pepper
- ❖ 1 teaspoon of garlic powder
- ❖ 1 teaspoon of onion powder
- ❖ 1 teaspoon of smoked paprika
- ❖ 1 teaspoon of chili powder
- ❖ 1 teaspoon of parsley, dried
- ❖ 8 bacon strips, thin

Directions:

1. Preheat the oven to about 200 degrees C and get a medium bowl and inside mix together the ground Beef with the spices.
2. Divide the mix into 8 different but equal parts. Line some 8 muffin cups with the bacon, in such a way that each cup will be circled by the strip of the bacon, then place each of the mini meatloaf inside the circle of within the strips of bacon.
3. Bake them for about 30 minutes and when done, simply transfer the cooked meatloaf unto some paper towels to drain before serving.

Calories: 290   **Protein: 11.4g**   **Carbs: 3.5g**   **Fat: 23g**

Beef and Broccoli Roast

Serves: 2
Prep Time: 10 mins.
Cook Time: 4 hrs. 30 mins.

Ingredients:
- ❖ 500g Beef chuck roast
- ❖ 100ml Beef broth
- ❖ 30g Soy sauce
- ❖ 1 teaspoon toasted sesame oil
- ❖ 1 bag frozen broccoli

Directions:
1. With the crock insert in place, preheat your slow cooker to low.
2. On a cutting board, season the chuck roast with pink salt and pepper, and slice the roast thin. Put the sliced Beef in your slow cooker.
3. Combine sesame oil, and Beef broth in a small bowl then pour over the Beef.
4. Cover and cook on low for 4 hours.
5. Add the frozen broccoli and cook for 30 minutes more. If you need more liquid, add additional Beef broth.
6. Serve hot.

Calories: 803   Carbs: 18g   Protein: 74g   Fats: 49g

Beef with Cabbage

Serves: 2
Prep Time: 10 mins.
Cook Time: 8 hrs.

Ingredients:
- ❖ 550g boneless Beef butt roast
- ❖ Pink salt
- ❖ 1 tablespoon smoked paprika
- ❖ 150g water
- ❖ ½ head cabbage, chopped

Directions:
1. Set your slow cooker to preheat on low.
2. Generously season the Beef roast with pink salt, pepper, and smoked paprika.
3. Place the Beef roast in the slow cooker insert and add the water.
4. Cover and cook for 7 hours on low.
5. Transfer the cooked Beef roast to a plate. Put the chopped cabbage in your slow cooker and put the Beef roast back in on top of the cabbage.
6. Cover and cook the cabbage and Beef roast for 1 hour.
7. Transfer the Beef to a baking sheet then shred with two forks.
8. Serve the shredded Beef hot with the cooked cabbage.
9. Reserve the liquid from your slow cooker to remoisten the Beef and cabbage when reheating leftovers.

Calories: 550   **Carbs: 10g**   **Protein: 39g**   **Fats: 41g**

Turkey Bacon Fat Bombs

Serves: 6
Prep Time: 1 hr.
Cook Time: 5 mins

Ingredients:

- 50g butter, cubed
- 100g cream cheese
- 80g turkey bacon
- 1 medium spring onion, washed and chopped
- 1 clove garlic, crushed
- Salt to taste
- Black pepper, to taste

Directions:

1. Add your cream cheese to a bowl with your butter. Leave uncovered to soften at room temperature.
2. While that softens, set your bacon in a skillet on medium heat and cook until crisp. Allow it to cool then crumble into small pieces.
3. Add in your remaining ingredients to your cream cheese mixture and mix until fully combined.
4. Spoon small molds of your mixture onto a lined baking tray, about 2 tbsp per mold. Then place to set in the freezer for about 30 minutes.
5. Set your Air Fryer to preheat to 190 degrees C. Add to your Air Fryer basket with space in between each and set to air fry for 5 minutes. Cool to room temperature.
6. When ready to serve, just spoon out 2 tablespoons, 30 g per serving. Store in the fridge for up to 3 days.

Calories: 108   **Carbs: 0.6g**   **Protein: 2.1g**   **Fats: 11.7g**

Spicy Mexican Casserole

Serves: 4
Prep Time: 15 mins.
Cook Time: 25 mins.

Ingredients:

- 650g ground beef
- 3 tbsp Mexican seasoning – you could use taco seasoning, fajita seasoning or Tex-Mex seasoning
- 85g butter
- 250g crushed tomatoes
- 230g grated cheddar cheese
- 55g jalapenos (pickled)
- 180ml sour cream
- 140g iceberg lettuce
- 1 chopped spring onion
- Salt and pepper for seasoning

Directions:

1. Preheat the oven to 200 C
2. Take a frying pan and melt the butter
3. Cook the beef until browned
4. Add the seasoning and the crushed tomatoes, combining well
5. Allow the mixture to simmer for 5 minutes and add a little seasoning if necessary
6. Take a medium baking dish and transfer the meat mixture into the dish
7. Add the cheese on top and the jalapenos
8. Place in the oven and cook for 20 minutes, until the top is brown and bubbling
9. Take a mixing bowl and combine the chopped spring onion with the sour cream
10. Serve the dressing at the side of the casserole

Calories: 840   **Carbs: 8g**   **Protein:50g**   **Fats: 66g**

Chicken Caprese

Serves: 4
Prep Time: 15 mins.
Cook Time: 35 mins.

Ingredients:

- 650g boneless chicken breasts
- 230g sliced mozzarella cheese
- 2 tbsp olive oil
- 1 tsp Italian seasoning
- 0.5 tsp garlic powder
- 2 sliced Roma tomatoes (beefsteak tomatoes will also work well)
- 2 tbsp balsamic vinegar
- 11g fresh, sliced basil
- Salt and pepper for seasoning

Directions:

1. Preheat your oven to 190 degrees C.
2. Place the chicken on a plate and drizzle the olive oil over the top, coating both sides.
3. Take a small mixing bowl and add the garlic powder, Italian seasoning and salt and pepper, combing well.
4. Sprinkle the seasoning over the chicken, coating both sides.
5. Place the chicken into the refrigerator for 20 minutes.
6. Take a large skillet and use a medium to high heat.
7. Place the chicken breasts inside the skillet and brown on each side; this should take about 3 minutes on one side, before turning for another 3 minutes.
8. Place the skillet into the oven and cook for 20 minutes.
9. Once the chicken is cooked, top each chicken piece with the mozzarella and the tomatoes.
10. Place back into the oven for another 3 minutes.
11. Add a little basil onto each chicken breast and drizzle the balsamic vinegar over before serving.

Calories: 460   **Carbs: 5 g**   **Protein: 52g**   **Fats: 24g**

Tomato & Pulled Pork Salad

Serves: 6
Prep Time: 25 mins.
Cook Time: 6 hrs. 12 mins.

Ingredients:

For the pork:
- ❖ 900g pork shoulder
- ❖ 2 tbsp olive oil
- ❖ 1 tbsp cocoa powder
- ❖ 0.5 tsp cayenne pepper
- ❖ 0.5 tbsp black pepper
- ❖ 0.5 tbsp ground ginger
- ❖ 0.5 tsp fennel seeds
- ❖ 0.5 tbsp paprika
- ❖ 1 tbsp salt

For the salad:
- ❖ 3 tbsp olive oil
- ❖ 2 spring onions
- ❖ 550g cherry tomatoes

- ❖ 1 tbsp red wine vinegar
- ❖ 1 tsp salt
- ❖ 0.5 tsp ground black pepper

For the hummus:
- ❖ 60ml olive oil
- ❖ 35g sunflower seeds
- ❖ 3 avocados
- ❖ The juice of half a lemon
- ❖ 8g fresh coriander
- ❖ 1 clove of garlic
- ❖ 2 tbsp sesame paste (tahini)
- ❖ 0.5 tsp cumin (ground)
- ❖ Salt and pepper for seasoning

Directions:
1. Take a pestle and mortar and grind the pork spices and the cocoa powder.
2. Add the olive oil and combine once more.
3. Rub the mixture over the entire pork shoulder, ensuring everything is combine dwell.
4. Use a slow cooker to cook the pork. Set it for 6 hours on a low setting or 5 hours if using high.
5. Once cooked, shred with two forks and set aside whilst you arrange the rest of the salad.
6. Take a baking tray and line with baking parchment.

7. Cut the cherry tomatoes in half and arrange on the baking tray.
8. Combine the salad spices with a little seasoning and the oil.
9. Brush the mixture over the tomatoes.
10. Place the tray into the oven and cook for 15 minutes at 225 degrees C.
11. Transfer the cooked tomatoes onto your serving plate and add the chopped spring onions.
12. Add a little of the vinegar over the top and a little more soil over the top of the tomatoes.
13. Take the avocados and cut into halves, removing the skin and pits.
14. Blend in a food processor until smooth.
15. Add the lemon juice and a little more olive oil if you find the mixture is too thick, season and make sure everything is well combined.
16. Serve the salad and hummus at the side of the pulled pork.

Calories: 760   **Carbs: 9g**   **Protein: 77g**   **Fats: 55g**

Tasty Chicken Broth

Serves: 8
Prep Time: 10 mins.
Cook Time: 20 mins.

Ingredients:

- 1 shredded rotisserie chicken
- 1.9 litres of chicken broth
- 110g butter
- 2 tbsp minced onion (dried)
- 170g sliced mushrooms
- 2 minced garlic cloves
- 2 chopped celery stalks
- 2 tsp parsley (dried)
- 2 sliced carrots
- 140g sliced cabbage
- Salt and pepper for seasoning

Directions:

1. Take a large soup pot and melt the butter over a medium heat.
2. Add the celery, mushrooms, garlic, and dried onion. Cook for 4 minutes, stirring occasionally.
3. Add the broth, parsley, carrot, and season. Combine and allow to simmer until all vegetables are softened.
4. Add the cabbage and the chicken, combining well.
5. Allow to simmer for another 12 minutes, until everything is soft.

Calories: 508   **Carbs: 4 g**   **Protein: 33g**   **Fats: 40g**

Sausage & Tomato Soup

Serves: 4
Prep Time: 15 mins.
Cook Time: 30 mins.

Ingredients:

- 650g of your favourite sausage
- 350ml chicken broth
- 1 tbsp butter
- 1 diced red pepper
- 1 minced garlic clove
- 1 minced onion
- 120ml crushed tomatoes
- 0.5 tsp dried sage
- 0.5 tsp dried thyme
- 0.5 tsp red chili pepper flakes
- 120ml double cream
- Salt and pepper for seasoning

Directions:

1. Take a large skillet and cook the sausage, pepper and minced onion over a medium heat
2. After around 10 minutes of cooking, season and add the sage, thyme and red chili pepper flakes, combining well
3. Add the crushed tomatoes, chicken broth and the cream, combining once more
4. Simmer for around 20 minutes over a low heat. The soup should start to thicken
5. Add the butter just before serving and stir to combine completely

Calories: 527   **Carbs: 6 g**   **Protein: 33g**   **Fats: 41g**

Cheesy Bacon Fingers

Serves: 2
Prep Time: 5 mins.
Cook Time: 12 mins.

Ingredients

- 170g bacon, cut into long slices
- 230g halloumi cheese

Directions:

1. Preheat your oven to 225 degrees C.
2. Take the halloumi and cut it into 10 equal pieces.
3. Take the bacon slices and wrap one piece around each piece of cheese.
4. Take a baking sheet and line with baking parchment.
5. Arrange the cheese/bacon and place in the oven until browned on one side.
6. Turn and cook until brown on the other side.

Calories: 748   Carbs: 4 g   Protein: 52g   Fats: 57g

Tarragon & Garlic Steak Salad

Serves: 4
Prep Time: 10 mins.
Cook Time: 15 mins.

Ingredients:

For the dressing:
- ❖ 1 pressed garlic clove
- ❖ 0.5 tbsp Dijon mustard
- ❖ 80ml mayonnaise
- ❖ 2 tbsp water
- ❖ 0.5 tbsp dried tarragon

For the salad:
- ❖ 1 cucumber
- ❖ 1 avocado
- ❖ 230g cherry tomatoes
- ❖ 220g leafy greens

For the garlic steak:
- ❖ 900g sirloin steak, cut into chunks
- ❖ 3 chopped garlic cloves
- ❖ 2 tbsp butter
- ❖ Salt and pepper for seasoning

Directions:
1. Take a medium mixing bowl and whisk all the dressing ingredients together until smooth.
2. Place the dressing into the refrigerator until you're ready to serve.
3. Arrange your salad onto your serving plate, however you prefer.
4. Take a large frying pan and add the butter over a medium heat.
5. Once the butter has melted, add the steak and season a little.
6. Add the garlic after a couple of minutes and combine everything well.
7. Cook until the meat is brown; don't cook for too long otherwise the meat will likely become chewy.
8. Arrange the steak pieces on top of the salad, along with any of the juices left in the pan.
9. Drizzle the salad dressing over the top and eat whilst still warm.

Calories: 681   **Carbs: 6 g**   **Protein: 52g**   **Fats: 47g**

Spicy Salmon With Spinach

Serves: 4
Prep Time: 10 mins.
Cook Time: 20 mins.

Ingredients:

- 55g olive oil
- 120ml mayonnaise
- 650g boneless salmon fillets
- 1 tbsp chili powder
- 7g shredded Parmesan
- 450g spinach, fresh works best but frozen would also work well
- Salt and pepper for seasoning

Directions:

1. Preheat your oven to 175 degrees C.
2. Take a baking dish and grease with a little of the oil.
3. Place the salmon on the countertop and season to your liking before arranging inside the baking dish, with the skin facing downwards.
4. Take a small mixing bowl and combing the mayonnaise, chili powder, and cheese.
5. Spread the mixture on top of the salmon.
6. Place the dish into the oven and bake for 20 minutes.
7. Take a small frying pan and cook the spinach in the rest of the oil until wilted.
8. Serve the salmon with the spinach at the side.

Calories: 677   **Carbs: 2 g**   **Protein: 39g**   **Fats: 56g**

Creamy Chicken Wings

Serves: 4
Prep Time: 20 mins.
Cook Time: 30 mins.

Ingredients:

For the dressing:
- ❖ 60ml sour cream
- ❖ 80ml mayonnaise
- ❖ 60ml double cream
- ❖ 85g crumbled blue cheese
- ❖ 3 tsp fresh lemon juice
- ❖ 0.25 tsp garlic powder
- ❖ Salt for seasoning

For the chicken wings:
- ❖ 900g chicken wings
- ❖ 1 minced garlic clove
- ❖ 0.25 tsp garlic powder
- ❖ 2 tbsp olive oil
- ❖ 40g shredded parmesan
- ❖ Salt and pepper for seasoning
- ❖ 350g celery stalks

Directions:

1. Take a large mixing bowl and add all the dressing ingredients, apart from the blue cheese.
2. Take an immersion blender and combine everything until smooth.
3. Add the blue cheese and stir in with a spoon.
4. Place the dressing into the refrigerator until you're ready to serve.
5. Take a large mixing bowl and add the chicken wings.
6. Add the oil and the spices and toss everything together to ensure the chicken is fully coated.
7. Place the bowl into the refrigerator for half an hour.
8. Preheat your oven to 200 degrees C.
9. Take a large baking tray and line with baking parchment.
10. Arrange the chicken wings on the tray and cook for half an hour, until fully cooked and crisp on the outside.
11. Take a large mixing bowl and add the parmesan cheese and then the chicken.
12. Toss everything together until completely coated.
13. Serve the chicken wings with the dressing either over the top or on the side and the celery stalks on the side for dipping.

Calories: 830   **Carbs: 4 g**   **Protein: 50g**   **Fats: 67g**

Cheesy Italian Meatballs

Serves: 4
Prep Time: 10 mins.
Cook Time: 20 mins.

Ingredients:

- 450g ground beef
- 1 egg
- 3 tbsp olive oil
- 55g butter
- 60g shredded Parmesan
- 140g fresh mozzarella
- 1 can of whole tomatoes
- 200g fresh spinach
- 0.5 tbsp dried basil
- 0.5 tsp onion powder
- 0.5 tsp garlic powder
- 2 tbsp chopped fresh parsley
- Salt and pepper for seasoning

Directions:

1. Take a large mixing bowl and add the meat, egg, spices, a little salt and the parmesan. Use an immersion blender to blend everything together well.
2. Create meatballs with your hands, around the size of a golf ball.
3. Take a large skillet and add the oil, warming over a medium heat.
4. Cook the meatballs on both sides until they're golden brown.
5. Turn the heat down and add the can of tomatoes, combining well.
6. Allow to simmer for 15 minutes and keep stirring occasionally.
7. Season and add the parsley, combining once more.
8. Take a separate frying pan and add the butter over a medium heat.
9. Cook the spinach for 2 minutes, until wilted, seasoning as you go.
10. Add the cooked spinach to the meatball pan and combine well.
11. Serve the meatballs with the mozzarella torn into pieces on top.

Calories: 628   **Carbs: 5 g**   **Protein: 39g**   **Fats: 49g**

Dinner

Shrimp & Mushrooms

Serves: 5
Prep Time: 15 mins
Cook Time: 5 mins

Ingredients:

- 300g shrimp
- 280g white mushrooms
- ½ teaspoon salt
- ¼ cup fish stock
- 1 teaspoon butter

- ¼ teaspoon ground coriander
- 1 teaspoon dried cilantro
- 1 teaspoon butter

Directions:

1. Chop the shrimp and sprinkle it with the salt and dried cilantro.
2. Mix the shrimp carefully. Preheat the air fryer to 200 degrees C.
3. Chop the white mushrooms and combine them with the shrimp.
4. After this, add the fish stock, ground coriander, and butter.
5. Transfer the side dish mixture in the air fryer basket tray.
6. Stir it gently with the help of the plastic spatula.
7. Cook the side dish for 5 minutes.
8. When the time is over – let the dish rest for 5 minutes.
9. Then serve it. Enjoy!

Calories: 56   **Carbs: 2.6g**   **Protein: 7g**   **Fats: 1.7g**

Keto Shrimp Cakes

Serves: 6
Prep Time: 15 mins
Cook Time: 10 mins

Ingredients:

- 400g shrimp meat
- ¼ teaspoon salt
- 1 teaspoon chili powder
- 1 teaspoon ground white pepper
- 1 egg
- 1 tablespoon almond flour
- 1 tablespoon butter
- 1 tablespoon chives

Directions:

1. Chop the shrimp meat into the tiny pieces. Put the chopped shrimp meat in the bowl.
2. Sprinkle the shrimp meat with the salt, chili powder, ground white pepper, and chives.
3. Stir the mixture gently with the help of the spoon. Then beat the egg in the shrimp meat.
4. Add almond flour and stir it carefully.
5. When you get the smooth texture of the seafood – the mixture is done.
6. Preheat the air fryer to 200 degrees C.
7. Take 2 spoons and place the small amount of the shrimp meat mixture in one of them.
8. Cover it with the second spoon and make the shrimp cake.
9. Toss the butter in the air fryer and melt it.
10. Transfer the shrimp cakes in the air fryer and cook them for 10 minutes.
11. Turn the shrimp cakes into another side after 5 minutes of cooking.
12. When the dish is cooked – chill them gently. Enjoy!

Calories: 107   **Carbs: 2.6g**   **Protein: 9.1g**   **Fats: 6.1g**

Salmon Boards

Serves: 4
Prep Time: 10 mins
Cook Time: 10 mins

Ingredients:

- 120g bacon, sliced
- ¼ teaspoon salt
- ¼ teaspoon turmeric
- ½ teaspoon ground black pepper
- 120g salmon
- 1 teaspoon cream
- 80g Parmesan
- 1 teaspoon butter

Directions:

1. Take the air fryer ramekins and place the sliced bacon there.
2. Put the small amount of the butter in every ramekin.
3. Combine the salt, turmeric, and ground black pepper together. Mix it up.
4. Then shred Parmesan.
5. Chop the salmon and combine it with the spice mixture.
6. Place the chopped salmon in the bacon ramekins.
7. Add the cream and shredded cheese. Preheat the air fryer to 180 degrees C.
8. Put the salmon boards in the air fryer basket and cook the dish for 10 minutes.
9. When the salmon boards are cooked – they will have little bit crunchy taste and light brown color.
10. Serve the dish only hot. Enjoy!

Calories: 411   Carbs: 1.9g   Protein: 36.2g   Fats: 28.3g

Keto Tuna Pie

Serves: 8
Prep Time: 20 mins
Cook Time: 30 mins

Ingredients:

- 240g cream
- 130g cup almond flour
- ½ teaspoon baking soda
- 1 tablespoon apple cider vinegar
- 1 onion, diced
- 500g Tuna
- 1 tablespoon chives
- 1 teaspoon dried oregano
- 1 teaspoon dried dill
- 1 teaspoon butter
- 1 egg
- 1 teaspoon dried parsley
- 1 teaspoon ground paprika

Directions:

1. Beat the egg in the bowl and whisk it. Then add the cream and keep whisking it for 2 minutes more.
2. After this, add baking soda and apple cider vinegar. Add almond flour and knead the smooth and non-sticky dough.
3. Then chop the Tuna into tiny pieces. Sprinkle the chopped Tuna with the diced onion, chives, dried oregano, dried dill, dried parsley, and ground paprika.
4. Mix the fish up. Then cut the dough into 2 parts. Cover the air fryer basket tray with the parchment.
5. Put the first part of the dough in the air fryer basket tray and make the crust from it with the help of the fingertips.
6. Then place the Tuna filling. Roll the second part of the dough with the help of the rolling pin and cover the Tuna filling. Secure the pie edges. Preheat the air fryer to 190 degrees C.
7. Put the air fryer basket tray in the air fryer and cook the pie for 15 minutes.
8. After this, reduce the power to 180 degrees C and cook the pie for 15 minutes more.
9. When the pie is cooked – remove it from the air fryer basket and chill little.
10. Slice the pie and serve. Enjoy!

Calories: 156　　**Carbs: 2.7g**　　**Protein: 8.8g**　　**Fats: 20.3g**

Turkey Quesadilla

Serves: 2
Prep Time: 5 mins.
Cook Time: 5 mins

Ingredients:

- ❖ 1 tablespoon olive oil
- ❖ 2 low-carbohydrate tortillas
- ❖ 80g shredded Mexican blend cheese
- ❖ 100g shredded turkey
- ❖ 2 tablespoons sour cream

Directions:

1. In a large skillet over medium-high heat, heat the olive oil.
2. Add a tortilla, then top with half of the cheese, the turkey, the Tajin seasoning, and the remaining cheese. Top with the second tortilla.
3. Peek under the edge of the bottom tortilla to monitor how it is browning.
4. Once the bottom tortilla gets golden, and the cheese begins to melt, after about 2 minutes, flip the quesadilla over.
5. The second side will cook faster, about 1 minute.
6. Once the second tortilla is crispy and golden, transfer the quesadilla to a cutting board and let sit for 2 minutes.
7. Cut the quesadilla into 4 wedges using a pizza cutter or chef's knife.
8. Transfer half the quesadilla to each of two plates. Add 1 tablespoon of sour cream to each plate and serve hot.

Calories: 414   **Carbs: 20g**   **Protein: 29g**   **Fats: 35g**

Buttery Garlic Turkey

Serves: 2
Prep Time: 5 mins.
Cook Time: 40 mins

Ingredients:

- ❖ 2 tablespoons ghee melted
- ❖ 2 boneless skinless turkey breasts
- ❖ 4 tablespoons butter
- ❖ 2 garlic cloves minced
- ❖ 50g grated Parmesan cheese

Directions:

1. Set your oven to preheat to 180 degrees C. Choose a baking dish that is large enough to hold both turkey breasts and coat it with the ghee.
2. Pat dry the turkey breasts and season with pink salt, pepper, and Italian seasoning. Place the turkey in the baking dish.
3. In a medium skillet over medium heat, melt the butter. Add the minced garlic and cook for about 5 minutes.
4. You want the garlic very lightly browned but not burned.
5. Remove the butter-garlic mixture from the heat and pour it over the turkey breasts.
6. Roast the turkey in the oven for 30 to 35 minutes, until cooked through.
7. Sprinkle some of the Parmesan cheese on top of each turkey breast.
8. Let the turkey rest in the baking dish for 5 minutes.
9. Divide the turkey between two plates, spoon the butter sauce over the turkey, and serve.

Calories: 642   **Carbs: 2g**   **Protein: 57g**   **Fats: 45g**

Creamy Slow-Cooker Pork

Serves: 2
Prep Time: 10 mins.
Cook Time: 4 hrs. 15 mins

Ingredients:
- ❖ 2 pork butts
- ❖ 200ml Alfredo Sauce
- ❖ 40g chopped sun-dried tomatoes
- ❖ 50g grated Parmesan cheese
- ❖ 150g fresh spinach

Directions:
1. In a medium skillet over medium-high heat, melt the ghee.
2. Add the pork and cook, about 4 minutes on each side, until brown.
3. With the crock insert in place, transfer the pork to your slow cooker. Set your slow cooker to low.
4. In a small bowl, mix to combine the Alfredo sauce, sun-dried tomatoes, and Parmesan cheese, and season with pink salt and pepper. Pour the sauce over the pork.
5. Cover and cook on low for 4 hours, or until the pork is cooked through.
6. Add the fresh spinach. Cover and cook for 5 minutes more, until the spinach is slightly wilted, and serve.

Calories: 900   **Carbs: 9g**   **Protein: 70g**   **Fats: 66g**

Baked Garlic and Paprika Turkey Legs

Serves: 2
Prep Time: 10 mins.
Cook Time: 55 mins

Ingredients:

- 600g turkey legs
- 2 tablespoons paprika
- 2 garlic cloves minced
- 250g fresh green beans
- 1 tablespoon olive oil

Directions:

1. Set oven to 170°C.
2. Combine all your Ingredients in a large bowl, toss to combine and transfer to a baking dish.
3. Bake for 60 minutes until crisp and thoroughly cooked.

Calories: 700   **Carbs: 10g**   **Protein: 63g**   **Fats: 45g**

Juicy Barbecue Ribs

Serves: 2
Prep Time: 10 mins.
Cook Time: 4 hrs.

Ingredients:

- 500g pork ribs
- Pink salt
- Freshly ground black pepper
- 1 package dry rib-seasoning rub
- 50ml sugar-free barbecue sauce

Directions:

1. With the crock insert in place, preheat your slow cooker to high.
2. Generously season the pork ribs with pink salt, pepper, and dry rib-seasoning rub.
3. Stand the ribs up along the walls of the slow-cooker insert, with the bonier side facing inward.
4. Pour the barbecue sauce on both sides of the ribs, using just enough to coat.
5. Cover, cook for 4 hours and serve.

Calories: 956   **Carbs: 5g**   **Protein: 68g**   **Fats: 72g**

Steak Bibimbap

Serves: 2
Prep Time: 10 mins.
Cook Time: 15 mins.

Ingredients:
- ❖ 1 tablespoon ghee
- ❖ 300g ground beef, minced
- ❖ Pink salt
- ❖ Black pepper
- ❖ 1 tablespoon soy sauce

Directions:
1. In a large skillet over medium-high heat, heat the ghee.
2. Add the ground beef, and season with pink salt and pepper.
3. Use a wooden spoon, stir often, breaking the steak apart.
4. Stir while adding the soy sauce. Turn the heat to medium and simmer while you make the cauliflower rice and egg.

Calories: 261   **Carbs: 2.6g**   **Protein: 20.7g**   **Fats: 17.5g**

Sesame Pork and Bean Sprout

Serves: 2
Prep Time: 5 mins.
Cook Time: 10 mins.

Ingredients:

- ❖ 2 boneless pork chops
- ❖ 2 tablespoons toasted sesame oil divided
- ❖ 2 tablespoons soy sauce
- ❖ 1 teaspoon Sriracha sauce
- ❖ 100g fresh bean sprout

Directions:

1. On a cutting board, pat the pork chops dry with a paper towel. Slice the chops into strips, and season to taste.
2. Set a skillet with a tablespoon of oil over medium heat.
3. Add the pork strips and cook them for 7 minutes, stirring occasionally.
4. In a small bowl, mix to combine the remaining 1 tablespoon of sesame oil, the soy sauce, and the Sriracha sauce. Pour into the skillet with the pork.
5. Add the bean sprout to the skillet, switch to low heat, and simmer for 3 to 5 minutes.
6. Divide the pork, bean sprout, and sauce between two wide, shallow bowls and serve.

Calories: 366   **Carbs: 5g**   **Protein: 33g**   **Fats: 24g**

Beef Burgers with Sriracha Mayo

Serves: 2
Prep Time: 10 mins.
Cook Time: 10 mins.

Ingredients:

- 340g ground beef
- 2 scallions, white and green parts, thinly sliced
- 1 tablespoon toasted sesame oil
- 1 tablespoon Sriracha sauce
- 2 tablespoons mayonnaise

Directions:

1. Combine the ground beef with the scallions and sesame oil in a reasonably sized bowl then season to taste. Form the beef mixture into 2 patties.
2. Set a greased skillet over medium heat and allow to get hot
3. Once very hot, add the burger patties and cook until done, about 8 minutes, flipping halfway.
4. Meanwhile, in a small bowl, mix the Sriracha sauce and mayonnaise.
5. Transfer the burgers to a plate and let rest for at least 5 minutes.
6. Top the burgers with the Sriracha mayonnaise and serve.

Calories: 575   **Carbs: 2g**   **Protein: 31g**   **Fats: 49g**

Avocado & Tuna Salad

Serves: 4
Prep Time: 10 mins.
Cook Time: 0 mins.

Ingredients:

- 80ml olive oil
- 1 can of tuna in water
- 85g sliced red bell pepper
- 2 sliced red onions
- 2 quartered cucumbers
- 55g diced celery stalks
- 3 avocados, stones and pits removed, cut into eight pieces each
- 2 tbsp fresh lime juice
- Salt and pepper for seasoning

Directions:

1. Remove the tuna from the tin and drain, flaking with a fork.
2. Place all the chopped salad ingredients onto a plate and arrange to your liking.
3. Add the tuna on top.
4. Take a small bowl and combine the olive oil and lime juice to create a dressing.
5. Drizzle the dressing over the top and season to your liking.

Calories: 639   **Carbs: 7 g**   **Protein: 44g**   **Fats: 45g**

Mediterranean Pesto Chicken Casserole

Serves: 4
Prep Time: 10 mins.
Cook Time: 30 mins.

Ingredients:

- 650g chicken thighs – boneless
- 2 tbsp butter
- 80ml green pesto (you can also use red pesto if you prefer)
- 1 chopped garlic clove
- 85g pitted olives
- 300ml double cream
- 140g diced feta cheese
- Salt and pepper for seasoning

Directions:

1. Preheat your oven to 200 degrees C.
2. Cut the chicken into small pieces and season.
3. Take a large skillet and add the butter over a medium heat.
4. Cook the chicken until browned.
5. Take a mixing bowl and combine the pesto and cream until smooth.
6. Take an ovenproof baking dish and transfer the chicken inside.
7. Add the olives, garlic, and feta, combining well.
8. Add the pesto mixture and combine everything once more.
9. Place in the oven for 30 minutes.

Calories: 737   **Carbs: 6 g**   **Protein: 43g**   **Fats: 60g**

Artichoke & Spinach Soup

Serves: 6
Prep Time: 10 mins.
Cook Time: 10 mins.

Ingredients:
- ❖ 2 tbsp olive oil
- ❖ 1 x 400g can of artichokes, chopped
- ❖ 280g frozen spinach, thawed
- ❖ 1 chopped onion
- ❖ 2 chopped garlic cloves
- ❖ 950ml chicken stock
- ❖ 400g cream cheese
- ❖ Salt and pepper for seasoning

Directions:
1. Take a large soup pan/saucepan and add the olive oil over a high heat
2. Add the garlic and onion, cooking until soft
3. Add the cream cheese and combine, turning the heat to medium
4. Add the spinach and combine
5. Add the chicken stock a little at a time, stirring each time you add
6. Add the artichoke and combine once more
7. Turn the heat back up to high and allow to boil
8. Then, turn the heat down to a simmer for around 10 minutes
9. Season to your taste

Calories: 435   Carbs: 9 g   Protein: 19g   Fats: 34g

Meatballs In Onion Gravy

Serves: 4
Prep Time: 10 mins.
Cook Time: 20 mins.

Ingredients:

- 650g ground beef
- 60ml double cream for the meatballs, and another 325ml for the gravy
- 1 minced onion
- 1 egg
- 3 tbsp butter, plus an extra 2 tbsp for the gravy
- 3 thinly sliced onions
- 0.5 tbsp soy sauce
- Salt and pepper for seasoning

Directions:

1. Take a large mixing bowl and add the beef, 60ml cream, egg, minced onion, salt and pepper, combining well.
2. Use your hands to form into meatball patties, flattening them down slightly.
3. Take a large frying pan and add the 3 tbsp butter, cooking the meatballs for around 4 minutes on each side.
4. Once cooked, transfer the patties to an ovenproof dish (retaining the cooking juices in the pan) and place in the oven, cooking at 200 degrees C for up to 15 minutes more.
5. Add a small amount of water to the cooking juices and set to one side.
6. Take a frying pan and add the rest of the butter over a medium heat.
7. Cook the onions until golden.
8. Take a large saucepan and add the cooking juices, cream and everything that is left to create a sauce, combine well, and allow to simmer for 10 minutes.
9. Add the onions and season, combining well.
10. Remove the patties from the oven and serve with the gravy on the side, or over the top if you prefer.

Calories: 880   **Carbs: 16 g**   **Protein: 42g**   **Fats: 71g**

Bacon & Broccoli Quiche

Serves: 4
Prep Time: 10 mins.
Cook Time: 20 mins.

Ingredients:

- 110g bacon
- 120ml double cream
- 8 eggs
- 170g mozzarella cheese
- 110g broccoli florets
- 0.5 tbsp onion powder
- 0.5 tbsp Italian seasoning
- Salt and pepper for seasoning
- 1 tsp butter

Directions:

1. Preheat your oven to 180 degrees C.
2. Take a pie tin and grease with the butter – around 23cm in size should be sufficient.
3. Take a skillet pan and add the bacon, cooking over a medium heat.
4. Transfer the bacon onto a paper towel to absorb the grease.
5. Cook the bacon into small pieces and place to one side.
6. Take a mixing bowl and add the cream, eggs, Italian seasoning, onion powder and a little salt and pepper, combining well.
7. Add the broccoli and bacon into the pie tin.
8. Add the egg mixture and distribute evenly around the tin.
9. Sprinkle the cheese over the top.
10. Cook in the oven for 20 minutes.
11. Allow to cool before cutting into slices.

Calories: 509   **Carbs: 5 g**   **Protein: 32g**   **Fats: 40g**

Pizza Casserole

Serves: 6
Prep Time: 10 mins.
Cook Time: 35 mins.

Ingredients:
- ❖ 2 tbsp olive oil
- ❖ 120ml marinara sauce
- ❖ 450g ground sausage
- ❖ 280g chopped bacon
- ❖ 2 eggs

- ❖ 325g shredded courgette
- ❖ 110g cream cheese
- ❖ 220g grated mozzarella
- ❖ 80g grated parmesan
- ❖ Half an onion, diced

Directions:
1. Preheat your oven to 200 degrees C.
2. Take a large mixing bowl and combine the cream cheese, half the mozzarella, the parmesan, courgette and eggs.
3. Take a casserole dish and grease with a little oil or butter.
4. Transfer the mixture into the dish and cook for 20 minutes.
5. Take a frying pan and cook the bacon and sausage until brown.
6. Once the courgette crust is cooked, top with the marinara sauce and spread evenly.
7. Sprinkle the meat mixture over the top and add the rest of the mozzarella.
8. Cook in the oven for another 15 minutes and add a small amount of olive oil over the top before cutting into pieces for serving.

Calories: 761   **Carbs: 9 g**   **Protein: 44g**   **Fats: 60g**

Curry Stuffed Bell Peppers

Serves: 4
Prep Time: 10 mins.
Cook Time: 0 mins.

Ingredients:
- ❖ 260g cooked chicken breasts, cut into small chunks
- ❖ 2 red bell peppers
- ❖ 1 tbsp curry powder
- ❖ 120ml mayonnaise
- ❖ 1 sliced spring onion
- ❖ 4 lettuce leaves
- ❖ Salt and pepper for seasoning

Directions:
1. Take the bell peppers and cut into halves, lengthwise.
2. Remove the seeds and place the peppers aside.
3. Take a mixing bowl and add the spring onion, mayonnaise, curry powder and the chicken, combing well and season to your liking.
4. Insert a lettuce leaf into each of the bell pepper halves.
5. Add the chicken mixture inside, in equal amounts.
6. Season and enjoy!

Calories: 296   **Carbs: 3 g**   **Protein: 16g**   **Fats: 23g**

Garlic & Ginger Shrimp

Serves: 2
Prep Time: 15 mins.
Cook Time: 15 mins.

Ingredients:

- ❖ 2 tbsp coconut oil
- ❖ 300g jumbo shrimps, prepared with tails on, peeled and deveined
- ❖ 2 chopped garlic cloves
- ❖ 2 tbsp chopped fresh ginger
- ❖ 450g sliced cabbage
- ❖ The juice of 1 lime
- ❖ 2 tbsp soy sauce
- ❖ 8g chopped coriander
- ❖ 2 tbsp sesame seeds
- ❖ Salt and pepper for seasoning

Directions:

1. Take a large frying pan and add half of the coconut oil.
2. Once hot, add the ginger, garlic, and the cabbage and combine well.
3. Cook for a minute and then add just a small splash of water and combine once more.
4. Cook until soft and keep stirring every so often.
5. Add the soy sauce, coriander, lime juice and the sesame seeds, combining well.
6. Take another pan and add the rest of the coconut oil.
7. Cook the shrimp for around 6 minutes, until they're no longer translucent.
8. Arrange the cabbage mixture onto your serving plates and add the shrimp on top.
9. Pour the rest of the sauce on top.

Calories: 389   **Carbs: 12 g**   **Protein: 38g**   **Fats: 20g**

Mexican Chili Bowl

Serves: 4
Prep Time: 15 mins.
Cook Time: 35 mins.

Ingredients:

- 3 tbsp olive oil
- 800g ground beef (you can use ground turkey if you prefer)
- 240ml beef broth
- Half an onion, chopped
- 2 chopped garlic cloves
- 1 diced tomato
- 2 tbsp tomato paste
- 2 sliced jalapenos
- 2 tbsp chili powder
- 2 tsp smoked paprika powder
- 2 tsp cumin

Directions:

1. Take a large cooking pot and add the olive oil over a medium heat.
2. Add the garlic and onion and cook until both have softened.
3. Add the chili powder, paprika powder, and cumin and combine well.
4. Add the meat and break up into smaller pieces.
5. Cook for around 15 minutes, until browned.
6. Add the jalapenos, tomato paste and tomatoes and combine, add the broth and allow the mixture to reach boiling point, before turning down to a simmer.
7. Cover the pan and cook for at least another 10 minutes, combining occasionally.
8. Season according to your preference and serve in individual bowls.

Calories: 779   **Carbs: 8 g**   **Protein: 50g**   **Fats: 59g**

Chicken Burger With Spicy Dressing

Serves: 4
Prep Time: 10 mins.
Cook Time: 18 mins.

Ingredients:

- 450g chicken breasts
- 2 tbsp butter
- 120ml mayonnaise
- 1 minced garlic clove
- 2 tbsp minced jalapenos (pickled variety)
- 8 large lettuce leaves
- 4 slices of cheddar cheese
- Half an onion, sliced
- 1 sliced tomato
- Salt and pepper for seasoning

Directions:

1. Take a mixing bowl and add the mayonnaise, garlic, jalapenos and a little salt and pepper, combining well to create a dressing. Place to one side.
2. Cut the chicken breasts in half sideways on and season with a little salt and pepper.
3. Take a large frying pan and add the butter until melted.
4. Add the chicken and cook on both sides until completely done.
5. Turn the heat down and top the chicken with the cheese, cook until melted.
6. Arrange a large lettuce leaf on each of the 4 plates, top with the chicken, a spoonful of the dressing, and top with a slice of onion and a slice of tomato.
7. Add another lettuce leaf on top and eat as a burger.

Calories: 460   **Carbs: 3g**   **Protein: 31g**   **Fats: 35g**

Desserts

Blackberry Shake

Serves: 2
Prep Time: 10 mins
Cook Time: 0 mins.

Ingredients:

- 230ml heavy, whipping cream
- 120g cream cheese, at room temperature
- 1 tablespoon Swerve natural sweetener
- 6 blackberries, sliced
- 6 ice cubes

Directions:
1. Combine all your ingredients in your blender and process until smooth.
2. Pour into two tall glasses and serve.

Calories: 407   **Carbs: 13g**   **Protein: 4g**   **Fats: 42g**

Root Beer Float

Serves: 2
Prep Time: 5 mins
Cook Time: 0 mins.

Ingredients:
- ❖ 1 can diet root beer
- ❖ 4 tablespoons heavy, whipping cream
- ❖ 1 teaspoon vanilla extract
- ❖ 6 ice cubes

Directions:
1. Combine all your ingredients in your blender and process until smooth.
2. Pour into two tall glasses and serve.

Calories: 56   **Carbs: 3g**   **Protein: 1g**   **Fats: 6g**

Mixed Berries Cheesecake Fat Bomb

Serves: 2
Prep Time: 2hrs. 10 mins
Cook Time: 0 mins.

Ingredients:

- 110g cream cheese, room temperature
- 2 teaspoons Swerve natural sweetener
- 4 tablespoons, ½ stick butter, room temperature
- 1 teaspoon vanilla extract
- 70g mix berries, fresh or frozen

Directions:

1. In a medium bowl, use a hand mixer to beat the cream cheese, butter, sweetener, and vanilla.
2. In a small bowl, mash the berries thoroughly. Fold the berries into the cream-cheese mixture using a rubber scraper.
3. Spoon the cream-cheese mixture into fat bomb molds.
4. Freeze for at least 2 hours, unmold them, and eat!
5. Leftover fat bombs can be stored in the freezer in a zip-top bag for up to 3 months.
6. It's nice to have some in your freezer for when you are craving a sweet treat.

Calories: 414   **Carbs: 9g**   **Protein: 4g**   **Fats: 43g**

Almond Fat Bombs

Serves: 12
Prep Time: 25 mins + freezing time
Cook Time: 5 mins

Ingredients:

- 5 tablespoon swerve
- 6 tablespoon almond butter
- ½ teaspoon vanilla extract
- ¼ teaspoon salt
- 6 tablespoon Erythritol
- 1 teaspoon stevia extract
- 8 tablespoon fresh lemon juice
- 3 eggs
- 1 teaspoon lime zest
- 2 tablespoon coconut oil

Directions:

1. Set your almond butter on to melt. Stir in your swerve once melted then whisk in your salt, vanilla extract, and Erythritol.
2. Transfer your mixture to your truffle mold then set to freeze.
3. While that goes, combine your coconut oil, stevia extract, lime zest and lemon juice then whisk well.
4. Whip your eggs and lemon mixture together using a hand mixer until smooth.
5. Set a deep pot on to boil then top with a metal mixing bowl to create a double boiler. Be sure that the mixing bowl does not touch the liquid.
6. Reduce to a simmer and pour your egg mixture into the mixing bowl, whisking continuously until curd it cooked (about 5 minutes). Remove from heat and set to chill.
7. Place the cooled curd into a piping bag then use it to stuff your fat bombs. Enjoy!

Calories: 120   **Carbs: 2g**   **Protein: 0.9g**   **Fats: 14.4g**

Cocoa Fat Bombs

Serves: 15
Prep Time: 10 mins
Cook Time: 5 mins

Ingredients:

- 90 g coconut butter
- 15ml cup extra virgin coconut oil
- 20g cup butter or more coconut oil
- 3 tbs unsweetened cocoa powder
- 15 to 20 drops liquid stevia
- Optional: 2 tbs erythritol or Swerve, powdered
- Optional: 1 tsp cherry, hazelnut, or almond extract, or pinch of cayenne
- pepper

Directions:

1. Let the coconut butter, coconut oil, and butter sit at room temperature to soften, but do not let melt.
2. In a food processor, combine all the ingredients but keep some cocoa aside for coating. Process until smooth.
3. Place a parchment paper and line it into a baking sheet. Use a spoon to form 15 small truffles. Place in the fridge for 30 to 60 minutes.
4. Remove the bomb from the fridge and sift the rest of the cacao powder over it.
5. Preheat your Air Fryer to 170 degrees C. Place the bombs in the Air Fryer basket with some space between each and let it cook for 5 minutes.
6. Cool to room temperature then store in the fridge for up to a week or freeze for up to three months.

Calories: 130   **Carbs: 2.7g**   **Protein: 0.9g**   **Fats: 14.4g**

Hot Chocolate Fat Bombs

Serves: 15
Prep Time: 10 mins
Cook Time: 5 mins

Ingredients:

- ❖ 15ml cup extra virgin coconut oil
- ❖ 20 butter or more coconut oil
- ❖ 3 tablespoons unsweetened chocolate powder
- ❖ 15 to 20 drops liquid stevia
- ❖ Optional: 2 tablespoons erythritol or Swerve, powdered
- ❖ Optional: 1 teaspoon cherry, hazelnut, or almond extract, or pinch of cayenne pepper
- ❖ 1/2 cup coconut butter

Directions:

1. Let the coconut butter, coconut oil, and butter sit at room temperature to soften, but do not let melt.
2. In a food processor, combine all the ingredients but keep some cocoa aside for coating. Process until smooth.
3. Place a parchment paper and line it into a baking sheet. Use a spoon to form 15 small truffles. Place in the fridge for 30 to 60 minutes.
4. Remove the bomb from the fridge and sift the rest of the cacao powder over it.
5. Preheat your Air Fryer to 170 degrees C. Place the bombs in the Air Fryer basket with some space between each and let it cook for 5 minutes.
6. Cool to room temperature then store in the fridge for up to a week or freeze for up to three months.

Calories: 145   **Carbs: 4.8g**   **Protein: 0.9g**   **Fats: 14.4g**

Peanut Fat Bombs

Serves: 12
Prep Time: 25 mins + freezing time
Cook Time: 5 mins

Ingredients:

- ❖ 5 tablespoon swerve
- ❖ 6 tablespoon peanut butter
- ❖ ½ teaspoon vanilla extract
- ❖ ¼ teaspoon salt
- ❖ 6 tablespoon Erythritol
- ❖ 1 teaspoon stevia extract
- ❖ 8 tablespoon fresh lemon juice
- ❖ 3 eggs
- ❖ 1 teaspoon lime zest
- ❖ 2 tablespoon coconut oil

Directions:

1. Set your peanut butter on to melt. Stir in your swerve once melted then whisk in your salt, vanilla extract, and Erythritol.
2. Transfer your mixture to your truffle mold then set to freeze.
3. While that goes, combine your coconut oil, stevia extract, lime zest and lemon juice then whisk well.
4. Whip your eggs and lemon mixture together using a hand mixer until smooth.
5. Set a deep pot on to boil then top with a metal mixing bowl to create a double boiler. Be sure that the mixing bowl does not touch the liquid.
6. Reduce to a simmer and pour your egg mixture into the mixing bowl, whisking continuously until curd it cooked (about 5 minutes). Remove from heat and set to chill.
7. Place the cooled curd into a piping bag then use it to stuff your fat bombs. Enjoy!

Calories: 134   **Carbs: 2.7g**   **Protein: 0.9g**   **Fats: 14.4g**

Strawberry Ketogenic Scones

Serves: 10
Prep Time: 10 mins
Cook Time: 20 mins

Ingredients:

- 190g of almond flour
- 20g of Swerve Sweetener
- 50g of coconut flour
- 1 tbsp of baking powder
- ¼ tsp of salt
- 2 Eggs
- 60g of heavy whipping cream
- ½ tsp of vanilla extract
- 150g of fresh strawberries

Directions:

1. Preheat your Air Fryer to a temperature of about 170° C and line your Air Fryer pan with a parchment paper.
2. Combine your salt, almond flour, coconut flour, baking powder and sweetener.
3. Add in your vanilla, eggs, and whipping cream; mold into a dough. Add in the strawberries and gently whisk.
4. Roll out the dough then cut into triangles. Transfer to your lined air fryer pan then set to fry at 180° C for about 20 minutes.
5. When the timer beeps, turn off your Air Fryer; then let the cones cool for about 5 minutes. Serve and enjoy your scones!

Calories: 154   **Carbs: 6g**   **Protein: 7g**   **Fats: 12.5g**

Blueberry Coconut Brownies

Serves: 6-7
Prep Time: 10 mins
Cook Time: 20 mins

Ingredients:

- 280g softened butter
- 4 tbsp granulated stevia
- 150g unsweetened cocoa powder
- eggs, Medium
- 1 tsp vanilla
- 150 g coconut, unsweetened, shredded
- 200g almond flour
- ½ tsp baking powder
- 60g blueberries

Directions:

1. Whisk together your butter and sweetener until fully creamed.
2. Fold in the remaining ingredients then pour into a lightly greased baking pan.
3. Set to air fry at 190 degrees for about 20 minutes.
4. When done, slice into squares then serve. Enjoy!

Calories: 183.5   **Carbs: 4.8g**   **Protein: 3g**   **Fats: 16.9g**

Ginger Biscotti

Serves: 6-7
Prep Time: 10 mins
Cook Time: 20 mins

Ingredients:

- ❖ 260g of whole almonds
- ❖ 2 tbsp of chia seeds
- ❖ 40ml of coconut oil
- ❖ 1 Large egg
- ❖ 3 tbsp of freshly grated ginger

- ❖ 2 tbsp of cinnamon powder
- ❖ ½ tsp of nutmeg
- ❖ A quantity of stevia
- ❖ 1 Pinch of salt

Directions:

1. Preheat your Air Fryer to 180° C. Process the almonds with the ginger and the chia seeds.
2. Mix your ingredients together in a bowl. Line your Air Fryer pan with a cooking sheet.
3. Form small biscuits and arrange it over your baking sheet. Place the pan in your Air Fryer and lock the lid.
4. Set the timer to about 15 minutes and set the temperature to about 180° C.
5. When the timer beeps; turn off your Air Fryer.
6. Set the biscotti aside to cool for about 10 minutes. Serve and enjoy your biscotti!

Calories: 152   **Carbs: 4.5g**   **Protein: 6.9g**   **Fats: 16.9g**

Hemp Cocoa Chocolate Fudge

Serves: 2
Prep Time: 10 mins
Cook Time: 20 mins

Ingredients:

- 2 tbsp of unflavored hemp protein powder
- 1 tbsp of cocoa powder
- 2 egg whites
- 1 tbsp of melted coconut oil
- 2 tsp of birch-sourced xylitol
- 2 tbsp of dairy-free divided chocolate chips

Directions:

1. Preheat your Air Fryer to a temperature of about 190°C.
2. Combine all your ingredients except for the chocolate chips in a mixing bowl
3. Pour the mixture in a steel ramekin or a heat proof ramekin.
4. Top the ramekin with the chocolate chips.
5. Put the ramekin in your Air Fryer basket and lock the lid.
6. Set the temperature to about 200° C and set the timer to about 20 minutes.
7. When the timer beeps; turn off your Air Fryer and set the ramekin aside to cool for 5 minutes.
8. Serve and enjoy your delicious dessert!

Calories: 173   **Carbs: 5.2g**   **Protein: 5g**   **Fats: 9g**

Egg Custard Tartlets

Serves: 8
Prep Time: 10 mins.
Cook Time: 25 mins.

Ingredients:

For The Tart Crust:
- ❖ 85g melted coconut oil
- ❖ 230g almond flour
- ❖ 4 tbsp erythritol (granulated)
- ❖ 1 egg
- ❖ A pinch of salt

For The Egg Custard:
- ❖ 6 egg yolks
- ❖ 425ml coconut cream
- ❖ 3 tbsp erythritol (granulated)
- ❖ 2 tsp vanilla extract
- ❖ 2 tbsp water
- ❖ 0.5 tbsp powdered gelatine (unflavoured)
- ❖ A pinch of nutmeg for serving

Directions:
1. Preheat the oven to 180 degrees C.
2. Take a medium mixing bowl and combine the almond four, 4 tbsp erythritol, salt, coconut oil and the egg.
3. Take a muffin tray and grease the bottoms.
4. Add the crust to the bottom of each muffin section, pressing down and up the sides.
5. Use a fork to prick holes in the bottom of each muffin section.
6. Place in the oven for 10 minutes and then allow to cool.
7. Take a medium saucepan and add the salt, remaining erythritol, cream, and vanilla, combine and allow to simmer over a low heat for 10 minutes, before placing to one side.
8. Take a small bowl and add the gelatine powder, adding enough cold water to activate and sit for 3 minutes.
9. Take another bowl and add the egg yolks, beating until they are pale and creamy.

10. Slowly add the coconut cream mixture into the eggs, using a whisk to combine constantly, until totally incorporated and smooth.
11. Transfer the mixture back to the pan and place back over a low heat.
12. Add the gelatin and stir for 5 minutes, until everything has dissolved and thickened a little.
13. Divide the custard mixture between the muffin crusts and place in the refrigerator until set, for at least 2 hours.
14. When you're ready to serve, dust a little nutmeg over the top.

Calories: 209   **Carbs: 7.7g**   **Protein: 8g**   **Fats: 15g**

Traditional Brownies

Serves: 24
Prep Time: 10 mins.
Cook Time: 25 mins.

Ingredients:

- 80ml almond butter
- 170g softened butter
- 160g erythritol
- 3 eggs
- 110g almond flour
- 2 tbsp water
- 30g cocoa powder

- 0.5 tsp baking powder
- A pinch of salt
- 1 tbsp vanilla extract
- 28g chopped dark chocolate (make sure the chocolate has 80% cocoa solids minimum)

Directions:

1. Preheat your oven to 180 degrees C.
2. Take a 23x33cm baking dish and line with parchment paper.
3. Take a large mixing bowl and add the almond butter, regular butter, erythritol and eggs. Combine with a stand mixer until smooth.
4. Add the almond flour, baking powder, cocoa powder, vanilla, salt and water, combining until smooth.
5. Add the chopped chocolate last and combine again.
6. Pour the mixture into the baking dish and smooth over the top.
7. Place in the oven for 24 minutes.
8. Allow to cool completely before cutting into pieces.

Calories: 121　　　**Carbs: 1 g**　　　**Protein: 3g**　　　**Fats: 11g**

Gingerbread Balls

Serves: 16
Prep Time: 10 mins.
Cook Time: 10 mins.

Ingredients:

- 140g almond flour
- 110g softened butter
- 1 tsp ground cinnamon
- 1 tsp ground cloves
- 1 tsp ground ginger
- 70g chopped roasted almonds
- 65g powdered erythritol

Directions:

1. Take a large mixing bowl and add all ingredients, except for the chopped almonds.
2. Use your hands to combine everything together until you get a smooth dough.
3. Place in the refrigerator to firm up for 20 minutes.
4. Again, use your hands to create smaller balls out of the dough, around 2.5cm in diameter.
5. Place the balls to one side.
6. Arrange the chopped roasted almonds on a plate.
7. Roll the balls into the almonds until all sides are completely covered.
8. Either eat immediately or place in the refrigerator.

Calories: 129   **Carbs: 1 g**   **Protein: 3g**   **Fats: 13g**

Lemon Cookies

Serves: 24
Prep Time: 8 mins.
Cook Time: 15 mins.

Ingredients:

- 325g almond flour
- 110g softened butter
- 120g cream cheese
- 110g erythritol
- 2.5 tbsp water
- 1 tbsp chia seeds
- 1 tsp vanilla extract
- 1 tsp lemon zest
- A pinch of salt
- 0.5 tsp baking powder

Directions:

1. Preheat the oven to 180°C.
2. Take a baking sheet and line with parchment paper.
3. Take a bowl and add the chia seeds with the water, combining and allowing to sit for 10 minutes.
4. Take another bowl and use a stand mixer to combine the erythritol and the butter, until a smooth mixture is created.
5. Add the cream cheese and combine once more.
6. Add the lemon zest, baking powder, vanilla, and chia mixture to the bowl with a little salt.
7. Use a slow mixing motion to combine into a smooth batter.
8. Use an ice cream scoop to transfer the dough onto the parchment sheet.
9. Flatten the mounds down slightly with the back of a spoon, until they're around 5cm in diameter.
10. Bake for 15 minutes, until browned.
11. Allow to cool before removing from the baking sheet.

Calories: 140   **Carbs: 1 g**   **Protein: 3g**   **Fats: 13g**

Keto-Style Tiramisu

Serves: 6
Prep Time: 15 mins.
Cook Time: 15 mins.

Ingredients:

For The Cake:
- ❖ 100g melted butter
- ❖ 140g almond flour
- ❖ 4 eggs
- ❖ 130g powdered erythritol
- ❖ 1 tsp baking powder

For the cream:
- ❖ 260g mascarpone cheese
- ❖ 4 tbsp powdered erythritol
- ❖ 475ml double cream
- ❖ 240ml coffee
- ❖ 4 tbsp cocoa powder

Directions:
1. Preheat the oven to 180°C.
2. Separate the egg yolks and whites and place into two separate, medium mixing bowls.
3. Use an electric mixer to beat the egg whites until stiff peaks form. Place to one side.
4. Add the 130g powdered erythritol to the egg yolk bowl and combine until yellow.
5. Add the baking powder and butter, combining well.
6. Add the flour and combine once more.
7. Use a plastic spatula to fold the egg whites into the flour mixture, carefully combining without overmixing.
8. Take a 9x13" baking pan and grease or use parchment paper inside.
9. Combine the dough mixture into the pan and place in the oven for 10-15 minutes.
10. Allow to cool before removing from the pan.
11. Meanwhile, take a separate bowl and whip the double cream until you see soft peaks forming.

12. Take another bowl and combine the remaining erythritol with the mascarpone.
13. Use a spatula to fold the cream into the mascarpone mixture.
14. Take a deep mixing bowl and add the coffee.
15. Cut the cake up into strips and drop them into the coffee-filled bowl, before transferring them into the bottom of your serving dish.
16. Add a layer of the mascarpone cream on top.
17. Soak more of the cake strips in the coffee and add another layer on top of the cream.
18. Add another layer of mascarpone cream.
19. Sprinkle the cocoa power on top and place in the refrigerator for 3 hours before serving.

Calories: 747   **Carbs: 6 g**   **Protein: 14g**   **Fats: 75g**

Bread

Coconut Flax Bread

Serves: 10
Prep Time: 10 mins.
Cook Time: 45 mins

Ingredients:

- ❖ 320g Coconut flour
- ❖ 40g Flax seeds, ground
- ❖ 1 tbsp. Flax seeds, whole
- ❖ 1/2 tsp. Salt
- ❖ 1/2 tsp. Baking soda
- ❖ 4 Eggs, pastured, beaten
- ❖ 2 tsp. Honey
- ❖ 1/2 tsp. Apple cider vinegar
- ❖ Butter, for greasing

Directions:

1. Set your oven to preheat to 170 degrees C, and lightly grease a loaf tin with butter, then set aside.
2. Add all your ingredients to a large bowl and stir to combine.
3. Pour batter into loaf tin and set to bake until the top becomes hard and you can insert a toothpick, and it comes back out clean, about 45 minutes.
4. Allow to cool fully, serve, and enjoy.

Calories:143.9   Protein: 6.3g   Carbs: 5.1g   Fat: 12.2g

Cauliflower and Almond Flour Bread

Serves: 10
Prep Time: 10 mins.
Cook Time: 30 mins

Ingredients:

- ❖ Cauliflower, 1 small head, chopped, roasted
- ❖ 50ml Olive oil, extra virgin
- ❖ 70ml Almond milk, unsweetened
- ❖ 6 Eggs
- ❖ 80g Almond flour
- ❖ 1/2 tsp. Baking soda
- ❖ 1/2 tsp. Salt
- ❖ 1 tsp. Garlic powder

Directions:

1. Set your oven to preheat to 190 degrees C, and lightly grease a loaf tin with butter, then set aside.
2. Add all your ingredients to a large bowl and stir to combine.
3. Pour batter into loaf tin and set to bake until the top becomes hard and you can insert a toothpick, and it comes back out clean, about 30 minutes.
4. Allow to cool fully, then serve.

Calories:108   **Protein: 6g**   **Carbs: 3g**   **Fat: 8g**

Whey Keto Bread

Serves: 6
Prep Time: 20 mins.
Cook Time: 30 mins

Ingredients:
- ❖ 12 Eggs separated
- ❖ 180g Whey protein, 1 cup
- ❖ Onion powder, ½ tsp

Directions:
1. Set your oven to preheat to 170 degrees C and prepare a loaf tin, preferably 9x5 by lining with parchment paper.
2. Crack your eggs and add it to your food processor then pulse until stiff peaks form.
3. Add remaining ingredients to food processor and continue to pulse until your dough is formed.
4. Add dough to a loaf tin and set to bake until the top becomes hard and you can insert a toothpick, and it comes back out clean, about 30 minutes.
5. Allow to cool fully, then serve.

Calories:99   Protein: 4.28g   Carbs: 2.42g   Fat: 8.51g

Keto Focaccia Bread

Serves: 12
Prep Time: 15 mins.
Cook Time: 20 mins.

Ingredients:

- 300g flax seed meal
- 1 tbsp. baking powder
- 1 tsp salt
- 2 tsp sugar
- 5 eggs
- 130 ml water
- 30 ml oil

Directions:

1. Set your oven to preheat to 190 degrees C and prepare a loaf tin, preferably 9x5 by lining with parchment paper.
2. Crack your eggs and add it to your food processor and pulse until fully beaten.
3. Add remaining ingredients to food processor and continue to pulse until your dough is formed.
4. Add dough to a loaf tin and set to bake until the top becomes hard and you can insert a toothpick and it comes back out clean, about 28 minutes.
5. Allow to cool fully then serve.

Calories:80.4   **Protein: 3.3g**   **Carbs: 3.2g**   **Fat: 6.8g**

Almond Breadsticks

Serves: 6
Prep Time: 10 mins.
Cook Time: 20 mins.

Ingredients:

- ❖ Bread stick base
- ❖ 200g mozzarella cheese
- ❖ 1 tablespoon Psyllium husk powder
- ❖ 1 large egg
- ❖ 1 teaspoon baking powder
- ❖ 3 tablespoons cream cheese
- ❖ 70g almond flour
- ❖ Extra cheesy
- ❖ 1 teaspoon onion powder
- ❖ 1 teaspoon garlic powder
- ❖ 20g parmesan cheese
- ❖ 10g cheddar cheese
- ❖ Italian style
- ❖ 1 teaspoon salt
- ❖ 2 tablespoons Italian seasoning
- ❖ 1 teaspoon pepper
- ❖ Cinnamon sweet
- ❖ 3 tablespoons butter
- ❖ 2 tablespoons cinnamon
- ❖ 6 tablespoons swerve sweetener

Directions:

1. Preheat the oven to 220 degrees C. Mix the cream cheese and the egg until slightly combined then set aside.
2. Combine all the dry ingredients.
3. Set your mozzarella cheese to melt using 20 seconds intervals in the microwave, stirring between each interval until sizzling.
4. Add in your eggs, cream cheese, and dry ingredients in with your mozzarella.
5. Knead to create a dough then set on a non-stick mat.
6. Press the dough flat until the baking sheet is totally covered with dough.
7. Transfer the dough to a foil using a pizza cutter to slice it.

Calories: 100   **Protein: 8.4g**   **Carbs: 3g**   **Fat: 14.2g**

Note: never use sharp objects and knives on a non-stick mat. Cut the dough then season as per the ingredient mentioned above. Bake for around 13-15 minutes on the top rack until crisp. Serve while warm with marinara or cream cheese butter cream, optional.

Garlic Breadsticks

Serves: 8
Prep Time: 30 mins.
Cook Time: 20 mins.

Ingredients:
Garlic butter:
- ❖ 60g Butter, softened
- ❖ 1 tsp Garlic Powder

Breadsticks:
- ❖ 200g Almond Flour
- ❖ 1/2 Tbsp Baking Powder
- ❖ 1 Tbsp Psyllium Husk Powder
- ❖ 1/4 tsp Salt
- ❖ 3 Tbsp Butter, melted
- ❖ 1 Egg
- ❖ 1/4 cup Boiling Water

Directions:
1. Heat your oven to 200 degrees C. Line your baking sheet with parchment paper and set aside.
2. Beat the butter with the garlic powder and set aside to use it for brushing.
3. Combine the almond flour, salt, baking powder and psyllium husk powder.
4. Add the butter along with the egg and mix until well combined.
5. Pour in the boiling water and mix until dough forms. Divide the dough into 8 equal pieces and roll them into breadsticks.
6. Place dough on baking sheet, allow to bake for 15 minutes. Brush the breadsticks with the garlic butter and bake for 5 more minutes. Serve warm or allow to cool.

Calories: 259.2   **Protein: 7g**   **Carbs: 6.3g**   **Fat: 24.7g**

Cheesy Cauliflower Bread Sticks

Serves: 2
Prep Time: 15 mins.
Cook Time: 45 mins.

Ingredients:

- 100g shredded mozzarella cheese
- 1 tablespoon organic butter
- 1 egg
- 1/2 teaspoon Italian seasoning
- 1/4 teaspoon red pepper flakes
- 1/8 teaspoon kosher salt
- 200g diced cauliflower, cooked for 3 minutes in the microwave
- 3 teaspoons minced garlic
- Parmesan cheese, the grated / powdered kind

Directions:

1. Preheat oven to 190 degrees C. Place the butter in a small pan and melt over low heat.
2. Add the red pepper flakes and garlic to the butter and cook for 2-3 minutes over low heat; don't let the butter brown.
3. Add the garlic and butter mixture to the bowl with the cooked cauliflower then add the Italian seasoning and salt to the bowl and mix.
4. Refrigerate for 10 minutes then add the mozzarella cheese and eggs to the bowl and mix.
5. Place a layer of parchment paper at the bottom of your 9×9 baking dish and grease with cooking spray or butter.
6. Add the egg and mozzarella to the cauliflower mixture. Add mixture to pan and smooth to a thin layer with your palms.
7. Bake for 30 minutes then take out of oven and top with some few shakes of parmesan and mozzarella cheese.
8. Cook for 8 more minutes then remove from oven and cut into sticks. Enjoy

Calories: 108   **Protein: 10g**   **Carbs: 6g**   **Fat: 24g**

Spicy Parmesan Breadsticks

Serves: 5
Prep Time: 20 mins.
Cook Time: 15 mins.

Ingredients:

- 1 head riced raw cauliflower
- 100g mozzarella cheese shredded
- 1 large egg
- 1 tbsp black pepper ground
- 1 tsp salt
- 100g parmesan cheese
- ½ tbsp Basil freshly chopped
- ½ tbsp parsley, freshly chopped Italian flat-leaf
- 70g mozzarella cheese shreded
- ½ tbsp garlic, 1/2 freshly minced

Directions:

1. Heat oven to 220 degrees C. Use a silicone baking mat or parchment paper to line baking sheet.
2. Mix ½ teaspoon black pepper, 1 teaspoon salt, ½ tablespoon fresh parsley, ½ tablespoon fresh basil, ½ tablespoon garlic, 1 egg, 100g parmesan cheese, 100g shredded mozzarella cheese and riced cauliflower in a suitable size bowl until combined and held together.
3. Place the above mixture to the lined baking sheet then spread it out to form a rectangle about 9x7" and 0.6 cm thick.
4. Bake in the oven for around 10-12 minutes then remove and top with the shredded mozzarella cheese.
5. Return to the oven and bake until the cheese melts and the bread begins to brown.
6. Leave it cool for about 10 minutes then slice into breadsticks. Garnish with parmesan cheese and fresh herbs.
7. Serve with your preferred red sauce and enjoy.

Calories: 100   **Protein: 8.4g**   **Carbs: 3g**   **Fat: 14.2g**

Cinnamon Swirl Bread

Serves: 10
Prep Time: 10 mins.
Cook Time: 40 mins

Ingredients:

- 230g Sunflower seed butter
- 50g Coconut palm sugar
- 3 Eggs
- 1 tbsp Vinegar
- 1/2 tsp Baking soda
- 1/4 tsp Salt
- 2 tbsp Stevia
- 1 tbsp. Cinnamon

Directions:

1. Set your oven to preheat to 190 degrees C and prepare a loaf tin, preferably 9x5 by lining with parchment paper.
2. Crack your eggs and add it to your food processor and pulse until fully beaten.
3. Add remaining ingredients, except stevia, and cinnamon, to food processor and continue to pulse until your dough is formed.
4. Add dough to a loaf tin, and sprinkle stevia and cinnamon on top.
5. Stick a knife directly in the dough and turn to create swirls throughout the dough.
6. Set to bake until the top becomes hard and you can insert a toothpick, and it comes back out clean, about 40 minutes. Allow to cool fully then serve.

Calories:90   **Protein: 4g**   **Carbs: 2.5g**   **Fat: 14g**

Nutty Garlic Bread

Serves: 10
Prep Time: 15 mins.
Cook Time: 25 mins.

Ingredients:

Bread Base:
- ❖ 170g Almond flour
- ❖ 1 tbsp. Coconut flour
- ❖ 3 Egg whites beaten well
- ❖ 2 tbsp. Olive oil
- ❖ 50 ml Warm water
- ❖ 1 tsp. Yeast granules live
- ❖ 1 tsp. Coconut sugar
- ❖ 120g Mozzarella cheese shredded
- ❖ 1/4 tsp. Salt

- ❖ 2 tsp. Baking powder
- ❖ 1/4 tsp. Garlic powder
- ❖ 1/2 tsp. Xanthan

Topping:
- ❖ 225g Mozzarella cheese shredded
- ❖ 2 tbsp. Butter melted
- ❖ 1/4 tsp. Garlic powder
- ❖ 1/4 tsp. Salt
- ❖ 1/2 tsp. Italian seasoning

Directions:

1. Set your oven to preheat to 220 degrees C and prepare a loaf tin, preferably 9x5 by lining with parchment paper.
2. Crack your eggs and add it to your food processor and pulse until fully beaten.
3. Add remaining ingredients, except topping ingredients, to food processor and continue to pulse until your dough is formed.
4. Add dough to a loaf tin and set to bake for 17 - 20 minutes or until the crust gets golden.
5. Add the topping ingredients and bake for another 17 - 20 minutes or until the top becomes hard and the cheese melts. Serve.

Calories:180   **Protein: 11g**   **Carbs: 4g**   **Fat: 17g**

Coconut Raisin Bread

Serves: 18
Prep Time: 10 mins.
Cook Time: 1 hour

Ingredients:

- 245g Coconut flour
- Raisins
- 80g Psyllium husk powder
- 1 tbsp Baking powder, gluten-free
- 1/2 tsp Salt
- 4 Eggs large, beaten
- 65g Coconut oil, melted
- 125ml Warm water

Directions:

1. Set your oven to preheat to 180 degrees C, then prepare a loaf pan, 9x5 preferably by lining with parchment paper.
2. Add your salt, psyllium husk powder, coconut flour and baking powder to a large bowl, and stir.
3. Add in coconut oil, eggs, and water then stir until just combined.
4. Pour batter in your prepared loaf pan and form a smooth round top, resembling your typical bread.
5. Set to bake until the top becomes hard and you can insert a toothpick, and it comes back out clean, about 60 - 70 minutes. Allow to cool fully then serve.

Calories:130.6   **Protein: 4.2g**   **Carbs: 2.8g**   **Fat: 22.2g**

Side Dishes

Garlic Bread

Serves: 20
Prep Time: 12 mins.
Cook Time: 1 hr.

Ingredients:

- ❖ 2 tsp cider vinegar
- ❖ 3 egg whites
- ❖ 140g almond flour
- ❖ 5 tbsp psyllium husk powder
- ❖ 240ml water
- ❖ 2 tsp baking powder
- ❖ 1 tsp salt, plus an extra half tsp for the garlic butter
- ❖ 110g room temperature butter
- ❖ 1 minced garlic clove
- ❖ 2 tbsp chopped fresh parsley

Directions:

1. Preheat your oven to 180 degrees C.
2. Take a baking sheet and line with baking parchment.
3. Take a medium sized bowl and mix the almond flour, psyllium husk powder, 1 tsp salt, baking powder, and egg whites, combining well.
4. Boil the water and add to the bowl with the vinegar and egg whites, using a hand mixer to combine for around half a minute. The dough should be like plasticine.
5. Wet your hands a little and separate the dough into 10 equal pieces.
6. Roll the pieces into sausage-shaped buns.
7. Arrange the dough onto the baking sheet and make sure that you leave enough space in-between as they will expand.
8. Place in the oven for 40 minutes and allow to cool.
9. Take a small mixing bowl and add the rest of the ingredients to form the garlic butter. Mix together and cover with plastic wrap, placing in the refrigerator for an hour.
10. Cut the buns into halves and add the garlic butter on each half, spreading evenly.
11. Turn the oven to 220 degrees C and place the bread back in the oven, for 15 minutes.

Calories:146   Protein: 3.8g   Carbs: 3.4g   Fat: 19.6g

Keto Corn Fritters

Serves: 4
Prep Time: 8 mins.
Cook Time: 6 mins.

Ingredients:

- ❖ 120ml coconut oil
- ❖ 2 tbsp coconut flour
- ❖ 100g cauliflower florets
- ❖ 1 egg
- ❖ 1 tsp fennel seeds
- ❖ A pinch of salt

Directions:

1. Take a food processor and blitz the cauliflower florets until you get a grain-like texture.
2. Take a bowl and add the coconut flour, the blitzed cauliflower, egg, fennel seeds and the salt, combining well.
3. Take a small frying pan and add the oil over a medium heat.
4. Use an ice cream scoop to take scoops of the mixture and add into the oil, frying until golden brown – do not cook more than three at a time, to give them enough space to move.
5. Once cooked on one side, turn and allow to cook on the other.
6. Remove from the pan and drain on a paper towel.
7. Repeat with the rest of the mixture.

Calories: 274   **Carbs: 1 g**   **Protein: 3g**   **Fats: 28g**

Healthy Kale Chips

Serves: 4
Prep Time: 5 mins.
Cook Time: 10 mins.

Ingredients:
- ❖ 1 tbsp olive oil
- ❖ 220g kale
- ❖ 0.5 tsp fresh lemon juice
- ❖ A pinch of salt

Directions:
1. Preheat your oven to 150 degrees C.
2. Give the kale a wash and pat dry.
3. Reserve only the large leaves and shred them into small pieces.
4. Take a large mixing bowl and add the lemon juice and a little salt.
5. Add the kale to the bowl and toss well to combine.
6. Take a baking sheet and line with parchment paper.
7. Arrange the chips on the sheet, leaving some space in-between.
8. Place in the oven for 10 minutes, until crispy but not burnt.

Calories: 49　　　**Carbs: 0.2 g**　　　**Protein: 2g**　　　**Fats: 4g**

Salmon & Prosciutto Skewers

Serves: 4
Prep Time: 10 mins.
Cook Time: 15 mins.

Ingredients:

- 450g salmon fillets, boneless and skinless
- 100g thinly sliced prosciutto
- 1 tbsp olive oil
- 11g chopped basil
- Salt and pepper for seasoning
- 8 wooden skewers, soaked in water

Directions:

1. Cut the salmon into pieces that are around 1.5 cm wide.
2. Thread the salmon onto each of the skewers.
3. Take a large plate and add the basil and pepper, mixing together.
4. Roll each of the skewers in the herb mixture, turning to coat evenly.
5. Wrap each of the skewers in the sliced prosciutto.
6. Brush each skewer with olive oil.
7. Take a large frying pan and add a little extra oil.
8. Cook until the salmon is cooked through, and the prosciutto has turned crispy, turning halfway and repeating the same.

Calories: 678   **Carbs: 1 g**   **Protein: 28g**   **Fats: 62g**

Cheesy Bacon Balls

Serves: 8
Prep Time: 8 mins.
Cook Time: 15 mins.

Ingredients:

- 1 tbsp butter, plus an extra 55g room temperature butter
- 140g bacon
- 150g cheddar cheese
- 140g cream cheese
- 0.5 tsp chili flakes

Directions:

1. Take a frying pan and melt the 1 tbsp butter over a medium heat.
2. Cook the bacon until brown and remove, placing on a paper towel to absorb the butter.
3. Cut the bacon into small pieces and set aside into a bowl.
4. Take a large mixing bowl and add the juices from cooking the bacon, along with the rest of the rest of the butter, two cheeses, and the chili flakes, season to your liking.
5. Use a whisk to combine everything well and place in the refrigerator for 15 minutes.
6. Once set, use an ice cream scoop to create 24 balls out of the mixture.
7. Roll each ball in the bacon pieces.
8. Serve immediately.

Calories: 283   **Carbs: 2 g**   **Protein: 11g**   **Fats: 26g**

Parmesan Cheesy Chips

Serves: 2
Prep Time: 5 mins.
Cook Time: 10 mins.

Ingredients:
- ❖ 60g grated parmesan cheese
- ❖ 2 tbsp whole flaxseed
- ❖ 2.5 tbsp pumpkin seeds
- ❖ 1 tbsp chia seeds

Directions:
1. Preheat your oven to 180 degrees C.
2. Take a baking tray and line with parchment paper.
3. Take a mixing bowl and combine all ingredients well.
4. Spoon a small amount of the mixture into mounds on the baking sheet, but make sure you leave enough space between and keep them raised, don't flatten them down.
5. Bake for 10 minutes but keep checking to ensure they don't burn; they should be golden brown.
6. Allow to cool on the tray before removing.

Calories: 263   **Carbs: 2 g**   **Protein: 17g**   **Fats: 19g**

Thank You!

Thank you for going through the book, I sincerely hope you enjoyed the recipes.

As I said before, a lot of time went into creating so many recipes and I really hope you're satisfied with the recipes provided.

I'm trying really hard to create the best recipes I can and I'm always open to feedback so whether you liked or disliked the book feel free to write on my email at deliciousrecipes.publishing@gmail.com.
I always reply and love to communicate with everybody. If you didn't like the recipes you can reach out and I'll share another cookbook or two for free in order to try to improve your experience.

I sincerely hope you'll like the recipes. Enjoy!

Printed in Great Britain
by Amazon